Mommy Mantras

*Affirmations and Insights
to Keep You
from Losing Your Mind*

Bethany E. Casarjian, Ph.D.
and Diane H. Dillon, Ph.D.

Mommy Mantras

• • • • •

Broadway Books
New York

BROADWAY

Broadway Books titles may be purchased for business or promotional use or for special sales. For information, please write to: Special Markets Department, Random House, Inc., 1745 Broadway, New York, NY 10019.

PRINTED IN THE UNITED STATES OF AMERICA

Visit our Web site at www.broadwaybooks.com

First edition published 2006

Book design by Elizabeth Rendfleisch
Illustrated by Susan McKenna/www.lillarogers.com

Library of Congress Cataloging-in-Publication Data
Mommy mantras : affirmations and insights to keep you from losing your mind /
Bethany E. Casarjian, Diane H. Dillon.— 1st ed.
p. cm.
Includes bibliographical references.
1. Motherhood—Religious aspects—Buddhism. 2. Parenting—Religious aspects—
Buddhism. 3. Mothers—Religious life. I. Casarjian, Bethany E. II. Title.
BQ5440.C37 2006
294.3'4441—dc22
2005053191

ISBN 978-0-7679-2380-4

1   3   5   7   9   10   8   6   4   2

*This book is dedicated with love
to our mothers and our husbands*

Contents

Mommy Mantras *n.* [derived from baby talk and Sanskrit.] **1.** invocations designed to transcend moments of mothering stress, fatigue, and anguish; side benefit to avert catastrophe befalling mother or child (or help put either party back together again). **2.** any combination of words that will summon compassion, composure, humor, and forgiveness toward an untamed mob, particularly between the hours of five and eight P.M. **3.** a way to reframe any mothering situation. **4.** affirmations to remind you that you haven't lost your mind.

Introduction

I would like to thank the people who came up with the idea of the "no candy aisle" at the supermarket. At the same time, I would like to know *why* they chose to pack those aisles with ten thousand other things my children would be willing to hurl themselves over a cliff for. Each week we are led like cattle into the holding chute of the checkout line. Rather than the torture of a branding (which is over far faster than unloading an entire cart of groceries), I am subjected to the whining and pleading of three expert wranglers. They circle me, and when they know I'm firmly pinned in the gates, they whip out the irons. "Please, Mom, just one pack of stickers," they begin. "Not today, honey. We came for food, not stickers." "Okay, then how about a balloon?" they ask, switching tack. "Can you eat it?" I ask. "No, but . . . ," they hesitate. There is a pregnant pause while they look for another strategy. Finally, as is sometimes the case, they place their money on screaming hysterics.

One of the children usually starts grabbing the contraband material as quickly as possible if he or she can reach it. Now I am in the position of getting him to relinquish it by invoking some brand of voodoo or snatching it forcefully from his steely grasp. All the while I am trying to unload the cart, find my credit card, sign the slip, and leave with some dignity. As I feel an increasing number of eyes on us, the stress tends to increase. On a bad day I ask myself, "Why do they *always* do this? *Where* did I go wrong? People must think I am the most pathetic mother ever." I tense up and start hissing threats through my teeth. I am trying not to attract attention, but it's way beyond that now. The person behind us bangs down her groceries pointedly to hustle the show along. Perhaps there is even a defining moment during the scene when the child hurls herself backward onto the floor, refusing to move.

As my anger starts to mount, I remind myself to take a few deep breaths. After my head stops reeling, I light on one of the stress mantras (such as *soften to the feeling* or *bring it on*) to help me reframe the situation. As I repeat the chosen mantra, my perspective starts to shift. I step back and see the situation more clearly. My anger doesn't seem so overwhelming. I feel a greater sense of control, and as a result, I become less reactive. By changing the script in my head, I alter my perception of the situation. Suddenly, I don't feel quite so squeezed in the chute. My feelings toward my children soften. I become more competent in dealing with their behavior, issuing consequences impartially, and defining my expectations for the next trip to the market—all this without maiming anyone physically or emotionally. At its best, a mantra has the power to help prevent these interactions from spiraling into toxic events that create lingering negative feelings toward our kids and ourselves.

WHAT MANTRAS CAN DO

Mine are not bad children. In fact, most of the time they are extraordinarily lovely and cooperative. But all children can push our buttons or make us entertain many drastic thoughts toward them. Often, without our full awareness, we devise negative scripts about ourselves or our children that undermine our ability to mother effectively. These statements deplete us and intensify our dark feelings. Sometimes these internal dialogues focus on our limitations rather than our strengths. Or perhaps we simply find ourselves unwilling to accept a situation for what it is and get locked into the pain of wishing it were something else. These negative statements and beliefs often intensify our criticism, shame, anger, judgment, and dissatisfaction, making the task of mothering even more difficult than it already is.

There's a lot about mothering that is beyond our control. As humans, however, we have an incredible capacity to change the way we think. Altering our thoughts, in turn, powerfully influences the way we feel and act. At the heart of Buddhism is the belief that all suffering originates in the mind. Psychologist Albert Ellis, the founder of Rational-Emotive Therapy, posits that our "self-disturbing thoughts" drive much of our emotional duress. Colleagues of Ellis's write: "We feel what we think. Events and other people do not make us 'feel good' or 'feel bad'; we do it ourselves, cognitively. It is as if we are writing the scripts for our emotional reactions, although we are not usually conscious of doing so." Of course, this begs the question, is there a way to change how we experience the hair-pulling challenges of mothering? Can one truly alter her feelings in the midst of the supermarket trip from hell? As a psychologist and mother, I believe so. And something that has helped me is reflecting on and using the mantras in this book. Within each mantra is the simple though powerful opportunity to grasp that *there is always another way to see the situation*, a way that potentially offers greater peace, comfort, acceptance, and balance than our initial response.

WHAT MANTRAS CAN'T DO

Mantras, while beneficial, can't change the basic makeup of the job. Mothering will always involve long hours, heavy physical work, and the type of worry that could bring down an elephant if put into a dart gun. At the same time, mantras can provide instant coping strategies to help us safely manage extreme feelings. Mantras won't let you off the hook when all three children contract the stomach flu. But they will remind you that the feelings of exhaustion and fatigue are temporary. Mantras won't alter the sometimes challenging temperaments of our children. Yet they can help reframe how we perceive and interact with our children, thereby alleviating some of the judgment and distress we feel. Mantras won't make us failproof. They can, however, help us appreciate the overwhelmingly difficult nature of the job and move us toward self-forgiveness. And most certainly, the mantras in this book are not a cure or treatment for the deeper psychological or behavioral issues you or your children may be facing. Throughout the book, I urge you to seek professional help when necessary. The mantras are available to help you cultivate a sense of inner support and calm while you receive the type of intervention your family needs.

HOW TO USE THE MANTRAS

Just as there's no one right way to mother, there's no single way to use the mantras in this book. Nor is there any correct approach to reading *Mommy Mantras*. Start at the beginning and read through. Or skip to the mantras that apply to the specific mothering crises or issues you are facing at the moment. At times, you might try a mantra and find that it's not doing the trick. Typically, more than one mantra falls under each heading. If the first one doesn't cut it, go to the next one. Or consider flipping to an entirely different section and see if a mantra contained there is more effective. The book is written so that you can dip in anywhere relief seems most imminent. As a result, you may discover some overlap between the mantras. Certain themes such as reframing situations, surrendering, and forgiveness are woven throughout the book. Hopefully you'll find these "workhorses" of perspective-shifting useful in a multitude of situations. When all else fails, stick with the mantra that reminds you to breathe. Chances are, just breathing will help you avert tragedy and clear your head.

Often, several mantras can be used over the course of a single event. For example, imagine your child has been particularly nefarious on a given day. In order to manage any extreme feelings that arise after she decorates the refrigerator with nail polish, you may first opt for an anger mantra. If you notice that deeper, residual feelings about your child are at play during the event, explore whether a mantra that deals with how we see our children is called for. A forgiveness mantra might provide closure and allow you to release your judgments or anger toward your child. Finally, a self-forgiveness mantra never hurts. This may encourage you to apologize to your child for your possibly over-the-top reaction and then assist you in letting go of any condemning thoughts and feelings you're directing toward yourself. Any way that the mantras offer relief, reprieve, and a sense of calm (even temporary) in the midst of heavy-duty mothering is the way they are meant to be used.

On another note, you may have noticed that there are two authors of this book, yet it was written using the word "I" when we refer to ourselves. Rather than putting our initials after each story or assigning different chapters to one another, we decided to use the word "I" throughout the book to represent our collective mothering experiences. Although the particulars might change, most of the stories could have been lifted out of any mother's life. We figured *who* the story happened to was less important than *what* happened and the mantra that emerged from the experience.

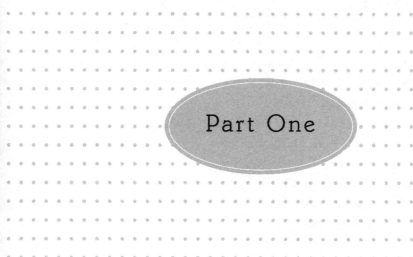

Part One

Mantras
to Lighten
the Load

You might be reading this book because you are a mother with considerable free time on her hands. But more likely you are reading it because, like any person trying to do the work of motherhood, you find yourself at times overwhelmed, stressed out, anxious, and furious beyond your wildest imaginings. Probably not all at once, but most likely all in one day. Mothering does more than test our mettle; it tests our sanity.

Anyone traveling with very young children may have entered

the darker side of mothering upon hearing a pilot say the following: "Okay, folks, it seems they're having a little weather in Chicago, so we're gonna hold tight on the Tarmac for a while longer. Good news is it shouldn't tack more than an hour onto flight time." You will most likely be seated behind a childless and punitive piano teacher who keeps turning the evil eye on you as your wailing child repeatedly kicks her chair. If you have more than one child, they will likely be clawing at each other over the armrest like deranged gerbils. And without fail, takeoff and descent will be punctuated by your child's shrieking response to ear pressure. Traveling on a commercial airliner with a baby or toddler is a true test for any mantra in this book.

But there's a deeper level to the darkness as well. We often don't tell each other how isolated, restless, inadequate, and generally "on the verge" mothering can make us feel. Nobody wants to be the mother who sometimes doesn't love her job. We swallow our dissatisfaction, then feel ground down. We worry whether we're good enough mothers and assume others are better. Surely it's easier for everyone else. Virtually every day I see a woman who looks as though she's handling the job with infinitely more grace and having much more fun than I am. There are periods when ordinary daily rituals can inspire an inner experience that is tantamount to a psychotic break. That's when I am sure that I'm missing some kind of nurturing gene.

Then I take a minute and look at it realistically. I think of my husband going to work while I stay at home to write this. He admits that he is sitting in a quiet office looking out the window in between bouts of productivity. But here there are children screaming at the door, trying to break it down to get at me. Why? It's unclear. But it is the same drive that requires them to be inside the bathroom when I'm in there. My daughter has a playmate over to the house who has pooped in her pants, requiring a full clothing overhaul, but she won't let the babysitter get near her, so it takes about thirty minutes out of my work time. And alas, our recently hired babysitter has learned that her college courses conflict with her days here, so she needs to quit. In an hour. So tomorrow, I'll be taking a three-year-old and a twenty-month-old to work.

In the larger scheme of things these are small problems, irritations, blips on the radar screen. But even these small disturbances can build up and leave you feeling depleted, stressed, and harried. And mothering carries big stressors as well—accidents, chronic illnesses, serious financial hardship. Add small problems on top of these larger conditions and it can all start to feel like more than we bargained for. It leaves you wondering whether other people are having these feelings. Can this be right?

Chapter 1

• • •

Managing Anger

Until I had children, I didn't think I had a temper. Any kind of temper. Pestilence, minor car collisions, my groceries put into someone else's cart *after* I paid for them, were met with an almost beatific composure. Having kids opened me up to a whole new side of myself. Buckling three uncooperative passengers in car seats when it is 105 degrees and watching them unbuckle "just to get something" can unglue a saint. This is especially true when you're already very late to go somewhere that is guaranteed to be equally unpleasant (e.g., dentist, doctor, town pool, grocery store).

Anger is the emotion that is most likely to "hijack" us, causing our reactions to be extreme and potentially harmful to our children. According to Daniel Goleman, anger is the emotion we have the hardest time controlling. In his book *Emotional Intelligence*, Goleman refers to our propensity to react hastily and "sloppily" when we're emotionally overstimulated as a "neural hijacking." This occurs when the amygdala, the brain structure responsible for processing and regulating emotions, becomes flooded and we explode with rage. This old neural circuitry, literally hardwiring us to act before we think, had its merits in the days when mere seconds in our reaction time determined our survival. Even though we rarely need to jump-start our bodies into action before sifting through the consequences, we often find ourselves "hijacked" by our anger. Unfortunately, these are the reactions we regret, the moments we wish we could do over or respond to differently.

Recently I was with one of my best friends, Lydia, right after she had her third child. All six of our kids were playing together. Lydia looked exhausted. Her baby was about four weeks old and her mother, who had been helping her, had left two days before. (I'm still not sure why she had us over there—sleep-deprived delirium perhaps.) Lydia's middle child, Eric, was not happy about the arrival of his new sister. And despite the extra attention from parents and grandparents, he continued to treat the baby roughly, pinching her when backs were turned. Periodically the air was punctured by his screaming loudly at her. Eric's behavior was a grab bag full of the nastiness that only a four-year-old who feels displaced and insecure can exhibit.

During the afternoon Eric continued to harass the baby by varying degrees. Lydia kept her cool. She spent time talking to him and soothing him. She preemptively separated him from the baby when he displayed menacing looks. I was in the adjoining room putting some train tracks together for the older kids when I heard a crash and the high-pitched wailing of a newborn. Later, I learned that Lydia had left the baby sleeping in her car seat and left the room for a moment. While she was gone, Eric had flipped the car seat over so that the baby was suspended upside down.

Lydia flew into the room, assessed what had happened, righted the car seat, and grabbed Eric by the shoulders. Without thinking, she started shaking him. I watched in empathic horror. I had been there emotionally. I understood, but she needed to stop. Momentarily, she caught herself and dragged Eric to his room. When she returned, she looked embarrassed and fragile. She began saying she shouldn't have done it, but she had just snapped, and she wished she had dealt with it better. Then she cried and cried a little more when she realized that the other children had watched her shake Eric. I told her the truth, which is that at some point, regardless of how we ended up dealing with those torrential feelings, we've all been there.

· The pump is primed ·

Research shows that we are most likely to have an intense anger reaction when we are already primed for anger. Lydia's repeated run-ins with Eric over the baby and her postdelivery fatigue had elevated her preexisting anger state. A good analogy is that if the anger well becomes too high, there's a threat that the water will spill over. In real terms it means we might let loose on our kid by doing or saying something we otherwise wouldn't have. Becoming aware of your internal anger state is a key preventative tactic. If you've had a rough day with multiple stressors, if you've been sick or more tired than usual, if there's something disruptive going on in your life, be aware. Notice whether your *pump is primed*. Just bringing your awareness to your internal state can often defuse a potentially explosive reaction.

If your anger *pump is primed*, bring your attention to it. Where are you holding the anger in your body? Are your teeth clenched? Take a moment to loosen your jaw. Is your breathing constricted? Take three deep and releasing breaths. Notice the tension wherever it is. For this mantra it is less important that you alter your anger than you become aware of it. As you go through the rest of the day, gently remind yourself that *the pump is primed*. See every other minor event with this knowledge. Knowing that you are already primed can often serve as a warning for you to bring greater awareness to each incident that happens. Knowing that *the pump is primed* can help you bring a broader perspective to the situation. Rather than snapping, you give yourself the space to consider how you might react, knowing that you are already emotionally charged. And sometimes just bringing this nonjudgmental awareness to the fact that you are primed can cause some of the anger to dissipate.

Here's an example of how it might work. You've asked your children to pick up the mess in the living room. Then you ask again. Instead of finding an industrious, cooperative agent of good, you find a surly eight-year-old who rails that you aren't the boss of him. Rather than launching into a tirade, it is possible to remind yourself that the *pump is primed*. This simple awareness automatically opens up your range of responses. You avoid the pitfall of screaming back that indeed you are the boss of him and you will be forever. Your behavior becomes intentional and voluntary rather than reflexive and conditioned. This simple awareness increases your control over how you react.

• This feeling is temporary •

No matter what feeling we are experiencing at any given moment, it won't last forever. Our rational, conscious brain knows this. But we often lose this knowledge and can't see a time when we might feel differently. Undeniably, our feelings exert tremendous control over us. Using the mantra *this feeling is temporary* is a way to reconnect to the fact that our emotions are constantly shifting. No matter how bad or strong a feeling is during any particular moment, rest assured it will start to shift as soon as we begin to experience it. Instantly reminding ourselves that a feeling is temporary at the onset can set the stage for the feeling to transform itself. The mantra *this feeling is temporary*, while not a cure for strong negative emotions, provides a cue for us not to get "locked in" to a feeling that is bound to change.

The mantra *this feeling is temporary* can be extremely beneficial when dealing with anger. Fury at finding permanent marker on the new couch becomes roiling anger, changes into steamy frustration, becomes self-judging for lackadaisical housekeeping practices and a firm resolve to lock up the markers, becomes an irritation, maybe becomes anger again when you realize you cannot afford to replace it or reupholster it, turns into feeling mildly perturbed, and finally becomes a remembrance. But the mantra *this feeling is temporary* can deter you from locking into a state of reflexive anger each time you look at the ugly black mark. Allow the possibility that the anger will soften from the get-go.

Breathe, now!

Sometimes we need a mantra that is capable of transforming more than just our perspective on a situation. This is particularly true for the moments when we become so intensely angered that we run the risk of losing control. Not long ago, two of my friends were at my house talking about how things have been really difficult for them at home. One was in the process of a divorce and the other was struggling with her son's bourgeoning behavior problems. All of our kids were in the living room playing happily until the dreaded exchange began. I call it the roping of the devil calves. It always goes the same way in our family. You gently but firmly call the child's name at the end of a visit to their friend's house and issue a five-minute warning. "Okay, honey, a few more minutes and then we're going to go." This is met with, "No, I don't want to go. I want to stay." You calmly reply, "Okay, I said five more minutes." Five minutes pass. You give yourself five more. Then you begin to herd the little calves. Again, you ask for their cooperation in retrieving strewn shoes and coats. You don't want to spook them. If they sense your fear, they'll scatter. If you are a novice, perhaps you think that your desire to leave or your need to "get dinner started" will spur action on the part of the child. If you are a worn confederate, you offer some incentive. "I'll let you watch one show when we get home." Sometimes this works, but often you've wasted your one good shot at the holding shoot.

Finally, after much cajoling and the outlining of consequences, you must physically approach the errant three-year-old and secure his or her fist while applying shoes. Maybe her own, perhaps not. Sometimes some pinning to the floor with a knee is involved. All three of my children have this bad leave-taking syndrome. I have followed through religiously on consequences (no playdates for a week, no public pool if that was the location of the botched leave), so things have gotten better, but I've seen it all—hiding under sofas, clinging to lamps. So eventually you rope the devil calves and make your way kicking and screaming out the door.

On this day, it was my friend's turn to do a little roping. Her initial approach was good, but she had a wild one on her hands. Beads of sweat appeared on my friend's face. She'd get a shoe on only to find it kicked off after she had moved onto the next one. She looked like she was going to have a stroke. And remember, you are doing this in front of your friends, which heightens the pressure. (Don't worry, there's a mantra for transcending the anxiety and stress caused by onlookers.) It's also hard to be the friend/observer at these times. Some of my friends are masterful commentators during ropings or other high-wire events. Responses tend to fall in the "I've been there" or "Hang in there" camps. But on this day, our other friend took the struggling mother's shoulder and said, "*Breathe, now.*" Her tone was perfect. That simple mantra defused our collective stress.

As the frustration mounts, it gets embedded in our body. Breathe it out. As the anger increases, we tense up and get rigid. As the drama and antics drag on, we create a tangle of nerves in our body right about where the heart sits. Breathing starts to untangle the cluster. The breath is like a conduit that releases the tension as soon as we bring our attention to it. In a sense, roping a struggling urchin to the ground is an exercise in futility. It's also a little degrading, even though we've all had to do it. But breathing is restorative. Urging our friend to breathe was an acknowledgment that her daughter's reaction was beyond our friend's control but her own breath was not.

Breathe, now! And our friend did. And it was good.

Chapter 2

• • •

The Blues

After having my first child, I jumped up out of bed—C-section be damned—climbed back up into my fifth-floor walk-up apartment, and acted as if nothing terribly out of the ordinary had happened with the exception of the baby arriving. Perhaps I'm exaggerating. Yes, I am. I was exhausted a lot of the time. My first son was so colicky that his pediatrician told me she used the sound of his screaming voice as her form of birth control. I was trying to finish my dissertation with the baby howling in the background. He never ate, and what he did eat he threw up shortly thereafter. It was not the easiest introduction to mothering, but I was fine. Perhaps because it was so hard, my expectations of what new motherhood would be like were shattered, and I surrendered all my other visions of domestic bliss and went into battle mode. And my particular crusade, or mantra if you like, was *do not kill this kid*. I remember feeling a great sense of purpose because I did have the patience to get through those first few nerve-grating months.

This was not the case after my second child. Upon her immediate arrival, I was convinced that I had made a catastrophic choice. I wept uncontrollably pretty much through the day. I thought I seemed okay to the outside world until my friend June asked me in a supportive and unabashed way, "Have you considered taking drugs to help you with that postpartum depression?" Huh, so it shows? Although most of my mother friends are more than happy to share at any given time all of the rage, judgment, disgust, and horror they feel toward their children, resulting in me feeling completely normalized regarding some of my darker moments, none of my friends had experienced postpartum depression. Not one. I questioned them carefully. I even explained the masked symptoms and read my diagnostic books to them. But I was the only one.

And it was worse with my third. I remember those weeks vividly. And the one thing I remember most is the feeling that I couldn't see the light at the end of the tunnel. I felt like I had made a choice there was no returning from, and that I had wrecked what good I did have. Looking back now, I wonder how I couldn't see that things always change. I had true tunnel vision, and this is a hallmark of depression. What seems unbearable now might look like a patch of the doldrums, or as in the case of some crises that occur in our lives, a transformative opportunity. But during that time all I could feel was an oppressive weight around my neck—the constant refrain that this black feeling was forever.

• This feeling is temporary—take two •

Looking back, I wished I'd had someone not only acknowledge that my depression was real, but really gotten through to me that it wasn't forever. The mantra *this feeling is temporary* can be a tool to push you past the intellectual knowledge that all feelings change and get you to a place where that understanding offers some real relief. If you find yourself in a tough phase of your life, take some time each day to repeat this mantra several times. Even if you don't feel like it or don't find it easy to believe at the moment, make saying it a regular practice. Close your eyes and allow yourself to be released, if only momentarily, from some of the sadness, depression, and loneliness you are feeling. Take three or four deep breaths and remind yourself that *whatever* feeling you are having at the moment, no matter how intense or powerful, *it is temporary*. It simply cannot last forever. No matter how dark the sky is with clouds, at some point a wind will usher them out. As you move through the depression or pain, visualize yourself getting closer to a lighter feeling. Imagine yourself steadily and constantly moving toward a time when you are not struggling with so much pain. And rest assured, no matter how long it takes, you *are* moving toward it

Important Note: Because my postpartum depression was mild, it abated after a few months. If you find yourself in a situation of postpartum depression or you're depressed even though you haven't recently had a baby, you may need to speak with your physician or another trusted health-care professional. There is much more awareness now about postpartum depression and depression in general. Help is out there. If you can't take this step yourself, confide in a friend and ask her assistance in getting the help you need.

I am hardwired for health

Something that helps reinforce the previous mantra is the knowledge that we as human beings are hardwired for health. My main area of interest as a psychologist is related to abused and neglected kids. One thing that continually amazes me are kids who suffer terrible maltreatment and actually function well, sometimes even thrive, despite the chronic abuse they experience. The scientific community refers to this as resilience, and it has garnered increased attention in the past twenty years. There is no clear formula that predicts which kids will demonstrate resilience, even though researchers have identified contextual and individual variables that are associated with it. But rather than being impressed by which kids demonstrate a tendency to thrive despite adversity, I am always struck by the fact that we as human beings are, in a sense, hardwired for health.

We have a natural tendency to develop along a healthy continuum. There are all types of interferences that can thwart or derail healthy functioning. But almost always there is the equally powerful inclination to heal, mend, and right ourselves. When we are spiritually or emotionally wounded, we often achieve a measure of equilibrium just through time. Knowing that we are predisposed toward health always makes me feel that no matter what type of blow motherhood or life deals out, chances are once I've gone through the initial stages of shock, grieving, desperation, or madness, I'm bound to be realigned with more tempered feelings as time goes on. I am reassured by our natural tendency toward health. So not only is *the feeling temporary*, but chances are your mind is already engaged in resolving the crises or conflict simply because that's how it works. We are *hardwired for health.*

· I am not this feeling ·

Sometimes feelings set in for extended stays, as with depression. Or for some of us, we have habitual and reflexive ways of dealing with certain events. One of my close friends struggles with anxiety. There is a long genetic line of anxiety and depression in her family, and it has been something she has contended with her entire life. College with its exams and other scholastic expectations was the first time she had a panic attack. After college she got a good job, things settled down, and her anxiety and occasional bouts with dysthymia (a milder version of depression) were relatively under control.

Once she had kids, however, her anxiety increased dramatically. She worried constantly about things that were within and out of her control. Money became more of an issue, and her marriage presented stresses that exacerbated her feelings of tension and worry. Whenever I spoke to her, it became clear that her anxiety, or "nerves" as she referred to them, was the lens through which she saw and experienced life. Her anxiety defined her. When I suggested that she might try to shift some of the ways she thought about the circumstances that triggered her anxiety, she looked at me with resolve and explained, "That's just who I am."

Finally, after much haranguing, she agreed to try the mantra *I am not this feeling* each time her anxiety got triggered. Upon recognizing the internal signs that her anxiety was rearing its ugly little head, she would do a full body scan, become aware of what sensations she was feeling, take three deep, full breaths, and say the mantra three times. It's not magic. All the mantra did was help focus her so that she was able to deal with the situation without completely internalizing the anxiety that came along with it. In a sense, it separated the feeling she was having from who she is at her core. *I am not this feeling* liberated her from having to react to the situation in her old conditioned way. Of course, if you are telling yourself you're an anxious person, you'll act anxiously. One would anticipate angry people to react with anger.

But reminding yourself that you are larger than any given emotion offers the potential to react with a greater spectrum of responses. It's easy with the enormous and often uncivilized demands of mothering to overidentify with our emotions and label ourselves as angry, fed up, or stressed. And while these may be a part of who we are at any given moment, the truth is that we are also much more. This mantra reminds us that there is another way of perceiving our emotions and ourselves.

With a lot of practice, we can develop to some degree the ability to stand back as a neutral observer of our emotions without constantly labeling them as good or bad. Through mindfulness practices such as meditation, we begin to develop the ability to experience our emotions while at the same time watching them in a more detached way. This doesn't mean you become detached from your life. On the contrary, you become more engaged by bringing your awareness to your thoughts, feelings, and behaviors. But you cultivate some distance toward your feelings and are able to notice what arises rather than becoming engulfed in them. As a feeling enters your consciousness you might say, "Ah, my old friend frustration" or "So, here's disappointment again." While this is difficult to do, it is worthy of the ongoing effort it requires. Over time this practice liberates you from being your feelings.

· · ·

Chapter 3

Monotony

My cousin Craig watched with growing tension as I filled up a water gun for what may have been the thousandth time during the hottest two hours of an August day. "For crying out loud, how long are you going to keep doing that?" he finally burst out. Just watching me perform this repetitive, apparently pointless task for a such a protracted period was more than he could take. At the age of forty-seven, Craig, a longshore fisherman, and his wife had adopted a two-year-old boy. With the arrival of the baby, Craig gave up fishing to become the primary caretaker. Gone were the days of perilous deep-sea adventure. Adios to the camaraderie of crewmates, the rush of repeatedly risking life and limb, and beating mother nature into submission. Hello diapers, tantrums, and cajoling a toddler to eat peas.

Whether he admits it or not, Craig was born to be a father. Calm, kind, patient, and loving, he's in his element. But the one thing about parenting a young child that still gets to him is how most of it is rather the same day after day. And with parenting, unlike fishing, when things get a bit dull you can't hoist up the sails and leave port. The following mantra is a reminder that resisting the monotonous moments of mothering only deepens our discomfort. The more we accept the mundane, the less aversive it becomes. Sometimes it even becomes joyful.

Surrender to the goat

One of my very good friends, Sarah, recently had a baby. I met Sarah years ago when we were both in one of our first clinical placements during graduate school. She is an amazingly competent professional, publishes scholarly articles regularly, and worked as a psychologist in the emergency room of a busy and rather frightening hospital. Unlike most psychologists, she encountered blood on a regular basis, which instantly raised her status as a mental health professional. Things that are challenging or impossible for other psychologists she treats with a kind of self-assured naturalness we all envy.

About ten months after she had her first baby, I was talking to her and she said, "You know, this is harder than I thought it would be." I asked her what was the most difficult thing and she replied, "the goat." I paused for a moment. Was she referring to her new baby? The pictures indicated a reasonably attractive infant. "What do you mean?" I asked cautiously.

"The damn goat at the zoo. Every day I need to get out of the house so I don't go nuts, and we walk to the zoo. And all he wants to do is sit in front of the goat pen and feed the goat. I have to pay fifty cents a shot to feed the goat. Every time I try to leave, he freaks out. So we sit there for hours. Well, it feels like hours and we feed the goat. I can't take much more goat." Of course she knew that she could take him somewhere else, but it would still involve feeding a goat—metaphorically.

So it was during this conversation that the phrase *surrender to the goat* was born. *Surrendering to the goat* takes on many variations such as *surrender to the building blocks* (the mantra of another friend), *surrender to the umpteenth reading of the only children's book in the collection that you don't like but your three-year-old loves,* and *surrender to dumping water from cup to cup in the tub.*

Our rational, educated adult minds often resist these repetitive and seemingly endless tasks. The harder we fight them, the longer and more unpleasant they seem. To counter our escape tendencies, spiritual guide Ekhart Tolle suggests, "Whatever the present moment contains, accept it as if you had chosen it. Always work with it, not against it. Make it your friend and ally, not your enemy. This will miraculously transform your whole life."

Despite our best intentions, it can be a true challenge to sit down with our children and completely surrender to the moment. I often begin an activity with my kids but find myself pulled away to the laundry, dishes, bills, or whatever else is on my agenda for the day. Part of that is just the reality of life—we have things to do. But another part is the autopilot pull to accomplish whatever mental checklist we have sketched out for the day.

For me what helps is setting aside a time for *surrendering to the goat*. In the evenings we all read together for about forty-five minutes. During that time I try hard not answer the phone or straighten up rooms. When my mind wanders to planning, thinking about chores I need to do, or even judgments about the present moment, I intentionally draw myself back. I listen to my oldest son read to us. I'm not always successful. Sometimes I avert all questions pertaining to the story and prod my son to get through the reading . . . must stay on schedule. But when I'm really there I feel my daughter pressed against my lap and hear the baby pad around us in a circle. Each time my awareness shifts from them, I gently bring it back.

In my own experience I have noticed that focusing on my desire to escape the moment intensifies its apparent unpleasantness. Our resistance to the moment becomes like treading water—we're already wet, but we're not gaining much from the exertion other than staying afloat. We also minimize the moment's potential for creating a real union with our child. For me, I can feel the power that bringing my total awareness to the moment creates. It's like we're in the zone. Time takes on a different dimension. We feel different because of it—all of us. But like anything, there are times that it's more difficult to truly be present. There are times when we need a mantra or a seed thought to get us through. And for those times, I remind myself that as tiring as this can be, it's short-lived and mind-bogglingly precious. I can see the need for more solitude already happening in my oldest son. And for Sarah, you might consider the longer mantra: *There is a small window in your child's life that will include a goat.*

Chapter 4

• • •

Stress

When my friend's son was born she thought he had an unusually large head, but she wasn't sure, him being her first baby. So she asked the pediatrician what she thought. The doctor looked at the baby and then back to my friend before she reassuringly said, "I'm sure there are bigger heads. I've never seen one, but I'm sure they're out there." That's a good analogy to how I perceive mothering. You could probably find a more stressful venture, but it's unlikely. At least it's unlikely that you'll find an occupation that is as *constantly* demanding and stressful as mothering.

There are lots of books and articles that document how stressful mothering is. I was reading a publication that detailed all of the physical and emotional detriments brought upon by mothering. It made me feel as though to be really decent to myself I should really get rid of my kids immediately. And there are many magazines and self-help manuals that present practical steps to reduce your stress load, including getting child care or housecleaning help (if you can afford it, which is another bag of snakes), making time for yourself, exercising, simplifying your schedule, and capping your kid's activities. All of these are great ideas, but they don't exactly reflect the spirit of this book. We know you have stress. And we know that there are really good reasons for why you have stress. And for as long as you are a mother, stressful conditions and events will continue to present themselves on a never-ending basis. Mantras won't eliminate the stress from coming down the river, but with practice they will help you dive underneath the waves instead of hitting them head-on.

· Within me there is a peacefulness ·
that cannot be disturbed

When my aunt, a seasoned meditation instructor and author on forgiveness, describes the utility of meditation, she likens it to being on the bottom of the ocean during a hurricane. The surface of the water is being torn by fierce winds and crushing waves, but at the bottom of the ocean, the storm is virtually undetectable. One of the side effects of meditating is that it cultivates an imperturbable space within you. Regardless of what's going on around you, it is possible to connect to a place that is centered and crisis-free. This place is not contingent upon your circumstances. Tapping into this reserve of calm and peacefulness does not require your life to actually be calm and peaceful. It doesn't really matter. The mantra functions in a similar way as meditation. It transforms the way you experience what is happening around you, and as a result changes your emotions and reactions.

Truth be told, I lifted this mantra from my aunt when I was about sixteen. The moment I heard *within me there is a peacefulness that cannot be disturbed*, I got it. What really appealed to me was the extremity of the statement. No matter what was happening in my life, I had the opportunity to emotionally inoculate myself from it. The locus of power shifted from being external to internal. Unlike with some of the other mantras, this one doesn't require much explanation. At any given moment, you have the ability to feel tranquil. Period. You may have to say the mantra several times. You may have to reassure yourself that while it might feel alien or bizarre to lay aside the anxiety, fear, and frustration that we often associate with stressful situations, it's fine to do this.

I think of *within me is a peacefulness that cannot be disturbed* as a mega-mantra. By that I mean that if you can really internalize its logic and power, you have the ability to radically alter the way you manage stress in your life. My other job, besides being a mom, is as a psychologist who works with incarcerated youth. I go into prisons and other institutions where adolescents are serving sentences and facilitate groups comprising about eight kids. I can honestly say that working with highly at-risk youth is a breeze compared to juggling day care, dinner, pickups, drop-offs, playdates, grocery shopping, and homework for the three I leave behind. It's like a glass pyramid that I pile up each day before I leave for work, and sometimes it feels as though there is someone standing outside who periodically slips in through the dog door to gleefully smash the thing in before I even get breakfast on the table.

When I was pregnant with my third child, I got locked in a prison because the inmate head count didn't add up. This happens periodically and is usually resolved within a half hour or so. But this went on and on for hours. The time I was supposed to be home to relieve the babysitter came and left. I was hungry and getting very agitated. I kept thinking how infuriating it was that I couldn't leave. I mean, really, what difference could my leaving possibly make in terms of them finding the person they may or may not be missing in the first place. As I began fuming about the state of the criminal justice system at large, I started feeling that not-so-comfortable feeling that passes over very pregnant women. For me it's part woozy, with slight vertigo and a touch of nausea. Not wanting to cause a scene, I started trying to breathe more deeply to calm myself down. Then I started repeating the mantra *within me there is a peacefulness that cannot be disturbed.* I'm sure I looked nutty, but I kept going until I really believed it. And I went a little longer until I felt it. And then I sat there. Each time the anxiety and stress returned, I repeated the mantra again. And as with most unpleasant events, it ended and I went home, where no one really even noticed I was that late.

• I can stand this •

Lisa's first child is quite winsome. Emma has an easygoing temperament and is almost pathologically cooperative. Not so with her second daughter, Lucy. She is a classic contrarian, though she is also charming, high-spirited, and wonderfully bold. So Lisa was lulled into a false sense of what the toddler years were really like. When things don't go Lucy's way, the fallout can be impressive. Lisa often becomes frustrated with Lucy's tantrums and screaming. She metes out ultimatums, time-outs, rewards for handling tantrum-inducing situations calmly, but at times there are twenty-minute bouts of screaming that set her nerves on edge. During one of these episodes, she called me on the phone and said, "I can't take this for one more minute." We talked on the phone for a while and I replied, "Sure you can. Look, you just did." And the fact is that *we can stand it*. We can stand almost anything. We may not like it, but we can tolerate it.

I can stand this is a pivotal mantra for stress because it literally lengthens our fuse. If you tell yourself that you can't stand something, it prompts you to alter the situation. Sometimes this is actually productive. If you tell yourself you can't stand the kitchen being a mess for one more minute, you might be motivated to clean it up. But if you tell yourself that you can't stand your infant's crying or your two-year-old's temper tantrum, you intensify your feelings of distress by resisting a situation that you can't necessarily alter. *I can stand it* empowers you to withstand anything without changing anything. You know that this will pass and you don't have to escape or obliterate anything for your emotional equilibrium. Telling yourself that you can't stand something confines your options by prodding you to react.

In the worst-case scenarios we shake our babies because we believe we can't stand the crying. We verbally degrade our children because we can't tolerate the feelings that arise in us as a result of their behavior. In these types of situations—get away from your child. If *the pump is primed* and the thought *I can't stand this* comes into your head, consider it a crisis and remove yourself. Put the baby in the crib. Lock yourself in the bathroom away from your eleven-year-old. Take a deep breath and remind yourself when you are ready, *I can stand this*. If you believe *you can stand it*, you can. If you're able to take a longer break to recharge yourself, do it. But the problem is that many of us are not in a position to remove ourselves for extended periods of time. If we could, the job wouldn't be so hard. That is why the mantra *I can stand this* is crucial. Try to ameliorate the most stress-provoking situations, but let's face it, mothering has its share of things we just have to tough out.

Kiss the ring

Kiss the ring is a slightly different mantra from *I can stand it*, though both involve distress tolerance. As I mention in the meditation chapter, one of the principal benefits of any mindfulness practice is its power to increase our ability to sit through difficult emotions. I know a man who teaches meditation to incarcerated adolescents. Each week they come to the group and sit silently for thirty minutes. When a pain arises in their foot, they are asked to sit through it until it abates. When restlessness arises, they are encouraged to observe the restless feeling without judgment or action until it passes. Studies have demonstrated that meditation does what traditional therapies often fail to do with this hard-to-reach population. Meditation increases these kids' impulse control and improves their ability to modulate difficult emotions—the ones that previously "hijacked" their amygdalas.

My friend Elsa told me about her personal mantra *kiss the ring* as it relates to dealing with her child's teacher. Elsa's youngest son has Down's syndrome. He also happens to have an above-average IQ, is very musically gifted, is lovely, warm, and completely full of piss and vinegar. His teacher was constantly pointing out to Elsa all of her child's weaknesses and shortcomings, never mentioning his myriad strengths. All in all, the teacher was abrasive and uncooperative, thinking more of her own comfort level than the emotional and educational needs of the child. But Elsa was savvy. Every time she had to interact with the teacher, she thought of it as *kissing the ring*.

In order to get what she needed for her son, Elsa had become an expert at finessing the system and smoothing the road to make her son's life easier. It reminded her of the good-hearted baker or tailor in the Mafia movies kissing the Don's ring to get something he desperately needed for a family member. *Kissing the ring* wasn't always pleasant, but it served her well. Elsa didn't view her actions as subservient or passive. Rather, she kept her gaze on the bigger picture. *Kissing the ring* helped Elsa depersonalize tasks that would have stopped others in their tracks, making her an extremely effective advocate for her child.

Elsa *kissed the ring* of the teacher continually that year, doing what she had to do to get her son through first grade as emotionally unscathed as possible. Rather than avoid interacting with the teacher because of the possible toxicity of the exchanges, she reframed it as a calling on behalf of her son. When he was safely in another teacher's class, she reported the old teacher to the principal, the teachers' union, and the PTA.

Increasing our distress tolerance is an essential mission for mothering and for living in general. Rather than trying to avoid or escape aversive emotions through overeating, drugs, overdrinking, overshopping, or anything else that temporarily numbs us, we learn to simply be with it. We attempt to take the pain as we take the pleasure. *Accept the hit as a gift. Kiss the ring* applies more to situations than to feelings. *I can stand it* pertains to our ability to endure distressing emotions with some degree of internal balance. *Kiss the ring* speaks to getting the job done, whether we like it or not.

· Soften to the feeling ·

Not long ago I was teaching a beginner meditation class for mothers when one woman began wincing and let out a small cry. A few minutes later she gasped and shrieked. I'm thinking to myself, "That's quite a tic you have there. But it's fine; maybe meditation will help iron some of that out or at least bring your *total* awareness to the tic." The meditation went on for about another fifteen minutes and when it was over, the other instructor asked the woman if she was okay, which I thought was rather bold and a little off-key given the fact that the tic was clearly beyond the woman's control. The woman said, "Acshoolly, I'm not. I haf a tewible toof'ache and the meditation was makin' me focus on it eben more." After the instructor sympathized with the woman, she asked her permission to lead her through a short meditation regarding her tooth pain in front of the class. The woman agreed, and this is what the meditation sounded like . . .

"Okay, if you will sit comfortably in your chair. Feel the backs of your legs against the chair. Feel your feet on the floor. Gently rest your hands on your thighs. Now go ahead and take three deep breaths. Feel the breath enter and leave your body, taking away some of the pain with each out breath. When you've finished, I want you to simply follow your breath. As you're doing this, you may begin to notice the pain arise in your tooth again. This time rather than fight the pain or judge the pain, I want you to try and *soften* into it. Each time the pain surfaces, instead of constricting your body, try and meet it gently and without resistance. Again, feel the pain and *soften* into it. Try not to judge the pain; instead just notice it as a physical sensation. You can think of the softening as melting around the sensation rather than hardening against it. Take a few moments to do this. And remember to stay with your breath."

As we all watched the meditation unfold, we could see from the woman's expression that she was still in pain. However, afterward she told the class that softening to the pain really worked. Each time it came up, she stopped fighting it and pictured it as gently floating around in her mouth. It still hurt, but it changed her subjective experience of the pain.

Softening to the feeling is something we can do with emotions as well as physical sensations. *Softening to the feeling* can also be described as a kind of radical acceptance of whatever the feeling is. The radical part is that we don't normally think of ourselves as willing to accept, acknowledge, or allow feelings that we experience as aversive or uncomfortable. But by *softening to the feeling*, we are discharging the negative power the emotion carries. We are neutralizing its force by altering the subjective way we experience it.

My husband often works long hours. We have three small children. Before I became hip to the fact that I would be solely responsible for taking care of these people all day long myself, I would create this little fantasy wherein my husband would leave work at a reasonable hour, walk in the door just as dinner was ending and the bedtime ritual was beginning, and take over for me while I cleaned up the kitchen. I would go so far as to cultivate this fantasy until the last possible moment—deep into dusk. To garner goodwill and avoid listening to me complain about quality-of-life issues all day long, he allowed me to believe that a reasonable return hour could happen and he encouraged me by claiming up until six o'clock that he might be able to catch an "earlyish" train. By seven-thirty I became angry and by eight I would light a fire under the cauldron of my indignation, which is always a nice thing for a spouse to return home to.

I realized that I had to do something to dissipate my bitter disappointment. I didn't want to be our friend's wife who called her husband's boss at two A.M. and began screeching that he better send her husband home now before she loaded the kids up and marched into the office to retrieve him. Many times I was close to that bad place.

The mantra *soften to the feeling* reminds me that when the disappointment arises, I don't have to seize up around it and make it the feeling I go to bed with. It doesn't have to be the way I greet my husband the minute he walks in the door. Instead of fighting the disappointment or getting frozen in it, I try to let the feeling surface while gently observing it for a moment. See it.

Soften around it. See it again, soften again, let it go. The minute my mind started to take off with the long internal monologue I created about raising these kids alone, the damage it is doing to them not to see their father, blah, blah, blah (not to imply that it's not a convincing story), I soften around the disappointment. As soon as I accepted the situation for what it was and the feeling for what it was, my mind stopped reeling. This doesn't mean that we accepted the larger situation. We found another job that was less demanding in a town where people don't regularly surrender their lives to their careers. But until that shift came, it was imperative for me to soften to the disappointment every time it arose. *Softening to the feeling* took away the dread and resentment that I (and my husband) came to expect every evening.

Bring it on

Periodically we reach critical mass. The stars align to throw every possible piece of bad luck your way. You see your grip on a situation start to slip as your universe spins rapidly out of control. Perhaps you try a few of the mantras already discussed in this chapter to shift your perspective and alter the way you experience the situation. It's like skiing on a mountain that is much steeper than you initially anticipated. A twinge of panic jolts your body and you realize that there is no way out. If you tense up and become fixated on resisting the difficulty of the trail, you will be swallowed up by the terrain. You are much better off throwing yourself into it, harnessing all of your capabilities, and rising to the challenge. Because I am often way over my head when I try to ski with my family and I have had several near-death experiences, I know this feeling well. I watch my family disappear below me and I realize that I am alone in all this. Standing on a tiny ledge of ice and looking down at what I am sure will be the site of my demise, I force myself to shift my attitude from a weak, fearful woman to that of a Nordic warrior. Over and over I say to myself, *Bring it on.* (Caution: This mantra, while useful for the initial launch from the perch, does not guarantee safety or success in the descent.)

Dinnertime in my house often rekindles the feeling that there's no way around it but through it. Critical mass is often achieved when the children have had tough days, dinner is late, and I am trying to accomplish another task. It becomes evident that the situation is not going to be neutralized and then transformed into a peaceful dining experience. Absent is any soothing conversation during which they recount their day at school while daintily dabbing crumbs from their chins. They are at odds with the world and with me. That's when I push the stray hair from my eyes, size them up, and mutter the mantra *bring it on.* This mantra is not a signal to crush or destroy the opposition; it is a cue to fully engage them on their turf. *Bring it on* can shape a negative event into a warrior act of service for a greater good. Think of it as being a really assertive monk.

Mindful parenting doesn't mean you always try to make everything nice and calm. This isn't always a pleasant job, and sometimes you have to step into the fire to forge the iron. The same is true for the other population I spend considerable time with. When I first starting working with highly at-risk kids, I struggled between using the voice of a student-in-training coming from graduate school and finding a language that, while still true to me, was genuine and accessible to my clients.

One of the first kids I worked with was a truly tough individual. He was almost seven feet tall. He used his size to intimidate others as a way to defend against the overwhelming fear and desperation he constantly experienced. This young man spent a lot of our early sessions swearing at me and threatening me. At the time, I was five months' pregnant and he desperately wanted me to be a mother to him rather than this baby. It made sense. After all, he knew me first. I wasn't really getting through to him until one day I abandoned my clinical reserve and emotionally and verbally met him in a place that he understood. I went to my supervisor shamefaced about how I had spoken to this client. Even though this departure felt liberating and joining, it didn't reflect what I had learned in graduate school to be the appropriate and balanced tone of a "professional." My very wise supervisor looked at me and said, "Hey, you're working with kids who have seen it all. They've been abandoned and abused. They have criminal records longer than most adult men in prison. Sometimes you've got to speak in a language they can understand."

My own children respond in the same way. On occasion, they need me to enter the arena with them. This doesn't mean that I set out to let boundaries slip or that I change my expectations for their behavior—respect and civility still apply for all. *But bring it on* lets me step up to the challenge so that I don't emotionally check out. It's a way to get your game face on and be superpresent. It also takes a lot of the resentment out of the equation. Rather than feeling put upon and enervated, I feel enlivened by the energy that accompanies the gauntlet being thrown down. Occasionally, to send the message of love you have to deliver it in a chariot of battle.

Chapter 5

• • •

Fear

My oldest son was thirteen months old when he had his first seizure. It was a Sunday night and I noticed he had a low-grade fever. I gave him some Tylenol and checked on him before I went to bed for the night. As I put my hand to his head, I noticed that his eyes didn't look quite right. I picked him up and he was limp and unresponsive. I called 911, and by the time they sent an ambulance he was in a coma. On the ride to the hospital, my mind started racing. "Will he live? And if he doesn't, how will I go on? I will never have other children, I can't bear this."

My close friend happened to be working that night in the ER. Penny is one of the attending pediatric physicians at Montefiore, and she is among the most grounded, stable people I have ever met. (With four children and a career you're either going to be a nut job or a monk—she's the latter.) As soon as I saw her face it became clear to me that to survive all of this I had to take each small moment at a time. I realized that if I left the reality of the situation and tyrannized myself with every catastrophic version of what might be, I was a goner. I asked her what was wrong with him and she said he was having a complex seizure, though the cause was undetermined. His fever was barely 100 degrees.

He was in a coma for three days, and each of those days I wasn't sure of anything. When my mind started spinning with questions, I tried to come back to the present. Would he come out of the coma? Would he live? Would he be my same baby as before? Each time these thoughts arose, I would gently bring my attention back to his moon face or his perfect hands. Time seemed to slow down and we were wrapped in the small cocoon of the hospital—suspended away from the rest of the world. Finally, on the third day he opened his eyes. We found that the cause of his fever was a common virus that he was likely to get again. Whether he would have such a severe reaction to this or any other fever-inducing virus was unknown. We saw some top-notch pediatric neurologists, all of whom had a wait-and-see attitude. From then on we were hypervigilant about his sleep, food, and exposure to sick kids. When he was eighteen months old, it happened again.

It wasn't any easier the second time because it wasn't possible to dismiss it as a fluke, a onetime deal. I thought, "Oh my God, this is my life." The neurologist encouraged us not to medicate him, saying, "I can live with this every six months." After some time I decided that I could, too. I was able to surrender to the fact that this was going to be a part of our lives, and that how we experienced not just the seizures and the hospitalizations but our daily lives in between those markers would be colored by how we decided to handle our anxiety and fear.

· Do what you can ·

Aside from the incomparable joy mothering offers, fear and worry create the other common ground. And to some degree, concern and anxiety for our child's well-being are all adaptive feelings. These emotions spur us beyond what I often consider to be human bounds to care for them when they are sick, stay awake when they are out late, drive them to appointments when you are near death with the flu. Fear and anxiety are carved deep into our mammalian brains for good reason. If they weren't, we might be tempted to abandon ship.

In fact, avoiding our anxiety regarding our children's well-being can be deleterious. To do so, we have to surrender a big part of our emotional awareness. I have worked with mothers who have severely abused and neglected their children. In order to psychically survive their actions, they have had to cut off from their emotional lives. Most of these women were already alienated from their feelings as a result of the abuse they experienced as children, which explains their behavior toward their own kids. But for most mothers, worry is part of the deal.

Do what you can is a mantra that clarifies for us what we can control and what we need to let go of. This is the mantra I used to cope with my son's seizure disorder. What I *could do* was watch him for fevers. I *could* give him medicine to control his fevers and make sure he napped, because sleep influences neural activity and indirectly affects the likelihood of a seizure occurring. I *could* even alert people he would be with of his condition and tell them what to do in an emergency. What my worrying and fear *couldn't do* was prevent a seizure from ever happening again. Each time I found myself slipping into a fit of hysteria (which was often), I would ask myself, *What can I do* about it now? And if the answer was nothing, I gently pulled my attention back to what was happening in the moment. Is he having a seizure now? Does he have a fever now? Is he overtired now? If the answers to these questions was no, then no action was required of me other than to reduce my anxiety by shifting my awareness back to the present.

Chapter 6

• • •

Letting Go of Negative Moods

In the past, anger management therapists would spend a lot of time "processing" clients' feelings of rage. People were encouraged to revisit issues or incidents that incited them. It was supposed to be a cathartic exercise to expunge angry feelings and clean the slate. At times, addressing feelings of anger and rage is still an important and beneficial therapeutic process. However, there is often little to be gained in ruminating endlessly over a past event that sent us over the deep end. It just makes us stew about it all over again. Recent anger work focuses on shifting clients' beliefs and thoughts about potentially anger-provoking situations in an effort to preempt or mitigate feelings of anger. They are then counseled to leave the anger behind rather than exhuming it. When angered, acknowledge it and move on.

The same can be said for other thoughts that trigger unpleasant feelings or memories. When these thoughts arise, acknowledge them and let them go. This approach does not advocate that you bury your head in the sand, refusing to confront problems or issues that need to be resolved. But rehashing old disagreements, conflicts, or tensions endlessly and without closure can drain the lifeblood out of us. Mothering offers us new opportunities to get incensed almost daily. We don't need to stew about old run-ins and irritations as well.

When it's over, it's over

There is a certain point in a physical struggle with a toddler when a horrifying realization washes over you. Undoubtedly it's going to spill. An impasse is reached. Shoulders lock, arms seize up, and each person's grasp tightens. Perhaps the object is a glass of purple grape juice on a white rug—perchance paint near a new tablecloth. In this case it was an industrial-size can of glitter. Few objects cause the level of consternation and dread that glitter can inspire in a mother. I know of homes where underneath the welcome sign it urges for all to heed, "Leave glitter at door." Good friendships between educated women are ended because of it. I'm not sure who slipped it into my daughter's possession, but somehow she had clawed the top off and began flinging it about like wildflowers in a laundry commercial. I dove onto her, but the moment I made contact with the glitter, her strength transcended the normal range of a three-year-old. She tried shrieking like a car alarm to disarm me. I countered with a jerking motion. She proved unflappable and hissed in an unsettling monotone, "Give it back."

This went on longer than one might have predicted from the physics involved—a grown woman against a child barely exceeding a squirrel in weight. Eventually, her brother came home from school and distracted her from the hysteria. But periodically she would look at me out of the blue and scream, "Give me back the glitter!"

A few hours later, she was sitting on my lap. I could feel the residual tension inside both of us. It was like we'd been in a fistfight. I felt resentful that we'd spent most of the afternoon locked in battle over colored bits of metal (plastic?). And she was furious that I robbed her of the glitter. (The fact that it's verboten only heightens the attraction.) I was left wondering what I could have done to circumvent the struggle. Probably nothing. Glitter happens. But by the end of the ordeal, I was extremely angry at her and frustrated with myself for losing patience.

The interesting thing was that at that very moment she swung around and told me that she really didn't like me *at all*. The event had a bad odor to it that we were surrounded by that afternoon, and we'd catch a waft of it periodically. When we were cooler, we talked about what happened. Then I made a conscious effort to let it go. I focused on bringing us both back to what was happening in the room at the moment. Not as a means of avoiding the experience, but to remind us both that ruminating doesn't undo the unpleasant events of the past.

Of all the mantras in the book, this one relates most directly to a pattern that has been a challenge for me. As my son likes to remind me, "You gotta just let that one go." For many of us, we conjure up the past not just to resolve an issue (which is often healthy and productive) but with a compulsive tendency to re-hash and relive it because it irritated us (which is a waste of time). The mantra *when it's over, it's over* is a reminder to me that bringing up old issues, reliving an anger-provoking experience, or trying to remedy a situation that has come and gone doesn't help.

When it's over, it's over is also a cue to release the physical residue of unpleasant past situations. As I was holding my daughter, it took a conscious effort on my part to let the anger, tension, and resentment go from my body. As I began to relax and move beyond our conflict, I saw her comportment change and soften (not that there's always a direct correlation between our moods and our children's). Taking a few deep breaths can help here. Breathing is a cue to our body to bring us back to the present moment.

When it's over it's over reminds us that similar circumstances might lead to very different outcomes. For the next couple of hours, each time she would begin to whine, I saw the beginnings of round two. I felt my body begin to tense and start to slip back into my defensive posture. Then my mind began feeding me stories of what was next. "Okay, once I say no again, she'll slide off my lap onto the floor. She's going to blow again. I'm in for another forty-five minutes of this. How long does this stage last?" Using the mantra allowed me to see the possibility that another fight was not necessarily a done deal. I could then see the past event as something that happened *but may not necessarily* happen again. By allowing this possibility, I made room for a wider range of options. I settled down in the present moment without being slavishly bound to the events of the past.

· Lock it in ·

It's one thing to be able to let go of the negative. It's the psychological equivalent of stopping the bleeding. But sometimes we need a transfusion—an influx of new blood. In the thick of mothering, it's not unusual to require an infusion of fortitude or a tangible reminder as to why we did this in the first place. You know the signs: shrieking at your children for minor transgressions, a look of dread painted on your face, the certain knowledge that you will not make it through bath time without reinforcements (and there are no backup troops). I'm not implying that in these moments we seriously question our decision to have children or lose touch with our devotion to them. But sometimes we need a heavy dose of the good stuff—joy.

Over the past two decades, researchers Doc Childre and Howard Martin have collaborated on the HeartMath program—a highly effective approach to managing stress, anxiety, and anger; strengthening the body's immune system; and reducing the chemicals associated with the aging process. What's unique about their approach to increasing emotional intelligence (or heart intelligence, as they refer to it) is the body of scientific data they have accrued to substantiate their work.

One of the fundamental steps in their technique asks people to "recall a positive, fun feeling and try to remember it." In a later stage, they train people to essentially "lock in" to that heart feeling for anywhere from five to fifteen minutes daily. Childre and Martin have demonstrated that "experiencing these core heart feelings (joy, appreciation, care, compassion, or love) is what provides regeneration to the nervous system, the immune system, and the hormonal system, facilitating health and well-being." The HeartMath studies repeatedly demonstrate increases in IgA levels (an important immune-functioning marker) in program participants.

Once you've let go of the stress, anger, and frustration that mothering can cause, take it a step further. Recall a moment, feeling, experience, or image that generates one of these heart feelings and *lock it in*. Maybe it's the maniacal look of happiness your three-year-old gets when he's on the swing. Or the joyful sight of your new baby sleeping soundly. Or the feeling of enormous relief when an older child returns safely for the night.

I remember shortly after having my third child, driving into Manhattan from our apartment in the Bronx to pick up my husband on Friday nights. Sometimes he would be working late, so we'd have to wait in the car. The best moments of my life were spent sitting there nursing the baby on a dark side street while the older kids drew pictures on the windows as they fogged up from our body heat. All my children were now in the world, in a car, safely parked on a snowy side street. A deep and irrepressible sense of well-being and contentment flooded me. (I'm pretty sure it wasn't just the nursing hormones, but even if it was, who cares?) Now when I need a fix, I think back to those nights. Then I let the feeling come back. And for as long as I can, I *lock it in*.

· I'm not Buddha ·

Of course there are many days when eight o'clock can't come soon enough. Having young children is physically demanding work and we're only human. Sometimes, even though we know that fully embracing the present moment will offer us relief, we cannot surrender. The mind is often a powerful adversary to our emotional well-being. It traps us into holding on to old familiar patterns and ways of tackling problems even when they are proven to be ineffective.

When you find yourself unable or unwilling to be totally in the present, when you are counting the seconds to bedtime, when a paralyzed look of dread and angst takes over your face for the last two hours of the day, remind yourself *you're not Buddha* (although you do have Buddha nature within you). There are days when getting through is good enough. In fact, it's better than good enough. It's incredible. All of these mantras are simply reminders that it's easier on us when we're present-focused. They're not meant to tyrannize us when we're not.

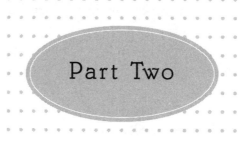

Part Two

Our
Children

Having children opened my heart like nothing else before it. Actually, it's more like they busted down the door with a giant log. I'm not saying I was an emotionless robot before having children—I cried at movies and slavishly adored our cat. But having children brought me to a new level of aliveness. Once the heart is open to that extent, we have access to an unimaginable degree of boundless compassion, joy, harmony, and unconditional love. Ready or not, your heart bursts open like a river spilling over its banks. Unfortunately, the swelling quite frequently extends the heart beyond its comfort zone. Flood warnings are issued regularly.

The flip side of such an awakening is that along with our profound love for our children, we often discover feelings that aren't easy to cope with. Some are unpleasant; others don't even seem rational. We may experience levels of anger, worry, resentment, and fear previously unknown to us. While the openheartedness of mothering is infused with enormous power to love, heal, and protect, it also has the ability to impact our children in less growth-enhancing ways. Because we love them so deeply, we risk identifying too closely with their pain, joy, successes, and failures. When the lines between *who we are* and *who they are* become blurred, we're on a slippery slope.

Recently, I was reading the Hans Christian Andersen tale *The Ugly Duckling* to my children. We were all troubled by the book. My kids were crying because of the baby bird's rejection, and I was cursing myself for choosing the damn book in the first place. Despite our discomfort, the story's universal appeal is clear and lies in the fact that we've all felt like outcasts at one time or another. Many of us still carry around these feelings of insecurity, of not measuring up, or of being deficient. Our culture's emphasis on competition, being the best, and achievement intensifies these feelings. And even when the conscious mind can dispel these deeply entrenched thoughts—we harbor the hidden fear that we really are a misfit bird. At times, we may even find ourselves projecting our unresolved feelings of inadequacy or failed aspirations onto our children without our full awareness—looking for them to compensate for our shortcomings.

Part Two of this book is an opportunity to examine who our children are both as autonomous beings and as individuals whose lives are deeply interconnected with ours. Embedded in mindful mothering is an ongoing requirement that we look honestly at how our own fears, wishes, and desires are coloring the way we perceive and interact with our children. As long as we are stuck looking at our children through the prism of our own unresolved issues or needs, we risk getting a distorted vision of who they *really* are. Beyond providing guidance, comfort, and safety, seeing our children is one of the fundamental tasks of mindful parenting. The mantras in this part of the book are designed to sharpen our vision and deepen our compassion for them and ourselves.

Chapter 7

• • •

How We See Them

While attending our first Lamaze class, the instructor asked us to write down one attribute we hoped our child would get from our spouse or partner. A simple question that opened a can of worms and started me thinking, "So, what *will* this new person be like?" Prior to this moment, I considered the baby to be like a small country I had colonized—possessing her own culture and climate, but residing within my domain. This question, however, made it clear that within weeks she would be released into the world as a free agent—a sovereign nation. I looked realistically at my husband and myself—reasonably intelligent, presentable, fairly athletic. So, what about the baby? Would this person inherit by some secret genetic code a love of dehydrated meats as her father and I share? Would we take one look at her and say, "Oh, she looks just like we thought she would?" Or, "I feel like I've known her my whole life?" No to all of the above.

The C-section after months of planning for a natural birth should have been a cue to get rid of all preconceived ideas about what was to follow. Then two things happened that completely unraveled the last thread of my pregnancy-induced fantasy. She was a boy. And he was the longest, blondest, skinniest baby I had ever seen. Where was the fat, ebony-haired newborn I had visualized? This child was already inches taller than I had been in the second grade. Of course, I couldn't have cared less what color hair or eyes the baby had. That all became irrelevant. I was happy to relinquish the fantasy in favor of the person that showed up that day.

Almost everyone has images or fantasies of what her children will be like. Some of these expectations are trivial and are dispelled quickly. But there are often expectations that are harder to surrender. By and large we anticipate our children will be healthy, we assume they will become attached to us, we expect that we will be able to meet their needs. When a child is difficult or ill, however, we often must modify our expectations of what raising her entails. Or perhaps we assume that this child will be similar to our previous children, when nothing could be further from the truth. When a child does not respond to us the way we had anticipated, we need to continually adjust our expectations in order to mindfully parent her. One of the great lessons of mothering is that our children come into the world with their own blueprints. No matter what we thought they would look like, act like, sound like, eat like, run like, or smile like, sooner or later we see that *they are who they are.*

· They are who they are ·

My cousin Nina spent her childhood making up musicals. She typically would present them to an unappreciative audience of family members who were eager to return to the predictable and reassuring entertainment of sitcom television. We were not a family who knew what to make of a child belting her heart out in a hand-fashioned pinafore, head scarf, and staff. Nina's original plan had been to enlist her cousins in rounding out the chorus. She soon realized that the costs outweighed any possible benefits of off-key singing and the constant refrain *"How long* do we have to stand here like this?"* Grown-ups would subtly check their watches to see if her performance was cutting into the beginning of the next half-hour slot of prime-time TV.

In college Nina joined the drama department, where she finally enjoyed the camaraderie of peers who could read music as well as set directions. Among her musically oriented peers she met and married a cellist. After having children, Nina would sing to them as her husband accompanied her on the cello. By the time they were in elementary school, her two oldest children could each play an instrument, were already mulling over which instrument they would study next, and knew every conceivable musical genre. Things went along smoothly until her daughter arrived.

My cousin's daughter, Amelia, will not stand for singing of any kind. She bays and howls for the radio to be turned off in the car like she's a dog being driven mad by a silent whistle. She refused to learn the alphabet because she "hates that song." In order to start her on the path to literacy, we recited the alphabet completely atonally with constant vows that we aren't trying to trick her with any melodic funny business. She often stares at us suspiciously as we tick off each letter in a monotone. Nina and her husband never hog-tied her and forced her to listen to Bach. Amelia just doesn't like music. Period. Initially, this was a blow to Nina. She just couldn't understand how a person doesn't *like* music. Sometimes she wondered if there was something wrong with her daughter. Perhaps she has hearing problems, she would ask hopefully. But my niece *is who she is,* and that means no show tunes.

To be fully present parents, we have to constantly resist the temptation to compare our children to anyone else. I have to quiet the voice in me that looks disparagingly and incredulously at my children as they roll on the floor screaming that they hate skiing *and* skating. When our parents innocently make notes of how our children are developing relative to their memories of our childhoods, I remind myself, *they are who they are.* When I get distressed that despite my best efforts, none of them has taken a shine to reading, I remind myself *they are who they are.* The quicker we relinquish the fantasy of who we thought they'd be and embrace the reality of who they are, the better off we are. I experience far more gratitude and peace of mind when I open up to the mantra *they are who they are.* And on some level, I'm sure they feel the difference, too.

Radically accept

I was jarred out of sleep in the middle of the night by a call from one of my closest friends. A few hours earlier Jane and her husband called from the hospital to let us know she had delivered a long-awaited baby girl. Now she was crying hysterically into the phone, explaining that shortly after birth the baby had turned blue and began having seizures. Clair, perfectly healthy in most regards, has a neurological disorder that resulted in her having multiple seizures almost hourly from birth to about eighteen months. At the age of five, she is virtually seizure-free, but her development is excruciatingly slow. Clair has learned to crawl, can feed herself, and is beginning to stand. And while she smiles and seems to understand speech, she does not talk.

The first year after Clair was born, Jane and George felt like they were trapped in a house of horrors. They sought out the best neurologists, looking for good news—or at least some encouragement that the seizures and the developmental delays caused by them would be outgrown. Like any of us would, they fiercely resisted the tragedy that had befallen their daughter and unconsciously believed that they could undo it by summoning enough willpower. But the more they resisted, the more they became entrenched in their suffering. As the enormity of the situation came into focus, Jane grew increasingly depressed. She became paralyzed by fear and anxiety about her daughter's life. Her friends offered support and compassion, but ultimately were helpless in alleviating her pain.

It didn't happen overnight, but during the next year, there was an extraordinary shift in the way Jane seemed to feel about her situation. Rather than resisting the reality of her daughter's condition and closing off to the world, she became *awakened* by it. Jane's entire demeanor changed. Before this transformation she seemed overwhelmed and defeated. Now she seems electrified by her mission. She is a woman on fire. We have watched in profound admiration as Jane has sought out traditional and alternative therapies for her daughter. As she describes new treatments I think, "How the hell did you even *think* of trying this? And how did you learn so much so fast?" She is polite, though thoroughly disappointed at my limited knowledge about brain structure, neurology, and cutting-edge treatments. "Didn't you have to learn *any* of this to get a Ph.D. in *psychology?*"

Jane is single-minded in her determination to help Clair but also attends to her own life, which includes nights out with her husband and being an incredible cook. Unlike most families who might have buckled under the pressure of caring for Clair while raising two normally developing children, Jane's family has thrived. They are miraculous. They are openhearted. We stand in awe of them.

As a psychologist it's always fascinated me how Jane manages what has been put on her plate. More than just getting by, she is so *happy.* Joyful, really. Part of it is her faith that God would not have made this part of her life for no reason. But there's more to it than that. Watching her over the past five years, I've come to suspect the key is her *radical acceptance* of her circumstances and her feelings. The act of *radical acceptance* is a spiritual practice and requires us to go beyond what we thought were our limitations. It requires us to embrace what may not be easy for us to accept on first glance both in terms of what is actually happening and our feelings in response to those events. Now, when fear, pain, frustration, or anger surface within Jane, she doesn't push them away or shame herself for feeling them. She accepts it all. Tara Brach, a psychologist and author on Buddhism, describes the heart of radical acceptance as "meeting whatever is happening within us with this kind of unconditional friendliness . . . Nothing is wrong—whatever is happening is just 'real life.' "

· Who's it really about? ·

Fay had not been particularly attractive as a young woman and it bothered her tremendously. She was the middle of three girls; her bookends were total hotties. Fay used her effervescent personality to attract people and she had a robust social life. However, she always wished she had been more of a true "tiara-wearing" beauty queen like her sisters. One homecoming queen sister is bad, but two is a cruel punishment. As these things happen, Fay's teenage daughter is a textbook bombshell. She's also socially precocious (read: a little wild). Since the age of fourteen, she has been pursued relentlessly by men of all ages. Many people have suggested to Fay that she handle Michelle's social agenda by tying a rope around the girl that stops short at the front porch. Contrary to this Draconian approach, Fay seems to passively encourage her daughter to date the best-looking, most socially adept boys around (read also: some trouble). It's clear, even to Fay, that the attention Michelle receives serves as a balm for Fay's buried adolescent ego. She says that each time her daughter receives attention for her physical attractiveness, it's an affirmation of her own beauty.

Fay's difficulty making peace with her physical awkwardness as an adolescent intrudes on her ability to mother mindfully at times, particularly in terms of limit setting. If Michelle breaks curfew after being out with a popular boy, Fay tends to skip the consequences part of the conversation and move right into the "*So*, how did it go?" Hidden in Fay's heavy investment in her daughter's social success and physical attractiveness is the risk that her daughter will overemphasize the importance of these aspects of herself—just as Fay has. Fay is a wonderful, loving, supportive mother. But her own unresolved emotions around this issue interfere with her ability to offer the balance her daughter needs to develop a healthy and cohesive sense of self.

I've certainly been guilty of living through my children's successes and failures. My oldest son's facility with numbers seemed like an excellent comeuppance to the algebra, geometry, and calculus problems that plagued me during my childhood. I felt delight when I realized he could add in his head, as I am still bound to counting on fingers. However, when I feel overly vindicated by my children's successes, it's often a call to be aware. Likewise, when I notice myself putting too much stock in how others perceive my children, the mantra *who's it really about?* helps me regain some clarity. Wishing our kids are the best, brightest, and most talented of the bunch usually has less to do with their adjustment and self-esteem and more to do with our needs for validation and approval.

For as long as we view our children as extensions or by-products of who *we* are, we tie our egos to their successes and failures. It's hard to be dispassionate observers of our children. We see flickers of ourselves in them. Periodically we might even find ourselves locked into reactive patterns with our children based on our own unresolved issues. The risk, however, is that we are not truly free to parent in the present. Both mantras—*who's it really about?* and *they are who they are*—speak to our children's autonomy and separateness from us. However, *who's it really about* asks us to go a step further. It asks us to examine our deep-seated emotional reactions to our children's behavior. *Who's it really about?* is a tool to question whether our responses are about our children's safety, well-being, and growth or whether they're tied to our own wishes, fantasies, desires, and sometimes even our feelings of inadequacy. We probably won't get rid of all our baggage before we have children. And mindful parenting doesn't require us to be perfect before we set sail. However, being aware of our issues and triggers can help us parent more consciously.

We all want our children to thrive. Appreciating their innate wisdom, beauty, and goodness is the cornerstone of *seeing* them. But loving our children, wishing them well, and attempting to minimize their suffering are not the same as being overly hooked into their performance. We breathe a sigh of relief when they are liked by their peers. My sister felt like she dodged a bullet when her son learned to read effortlessly after she struggled with dyslexia all her life. But sometimes, without realizing it, we look to our children to succeed where we have not.

It's not hard to see how our sense of self can trickle into our child's performance and behavior. We're raised to believe that our children are offshoots of us. A woman I know said that she never had children because "it's just too narcissistic." I'm not sure she completely captured the beauty and splendor of family life, but she had a point. For many of us, our child's capabilities, behavior, successes, and shortcomings serve as reflections of who we are as people and as mothers. When I find myself caring too much about my children's achievements or performances, it is a signal to me to ask *who's it really about?* I recently saw a woman crying at a peewee hockey game because her son didn't get to play on the starting line. I watched as the child sat on the bench, laughing with his friends and spitting water through the gaps in his teeth. Upstairs in the observation booth his mom cried her heart out, lamenting her son's loss. I wondered how happy he would feel after the game when he was reunited with his mom.

The mantra *who's it really about?* serves as a gentle reminder to look at some of the unresolved issues in our own lives. Unhealthy thoughts about ourselves almost always impinge upon our ability to accept our children's successes and failures with a certain amount of equanimity. The more we practice *radical acceptance* and compassion for ourselves, the less our children grow up in the wake of our fears and disappointments.

· Six of one . . . ·

Six of one is a mini-mantra. It's a reminder that truly mindful mothering extends to children who aren't ours. A very good friend of mine had a babysitter, Patricia, who became part of their family. Patricia, also known as the goddess of patience and all things good, brought her own daughter, Lilly, to work each day. My friend welcomed the little girl into her home not as a guest or a visitor, but with the spirit that she was simply one of the pack. She was both intentional and relaxed about this. She didn't force it or call undue attention to the fact. When she bought pajamas for her kids, Lilly got them. A day at the beach, Lilly went, too. When I mentioned once that she treated Lilly with the same warmth and attention she did her own, she shrugged her shoulders and said, "Yeah, *six of one*, half a dozen of the other." Her delivery may have been blasé, but her loving inclusiveness was far from it.

When I discover myself secretly wishing for my child's security or happiness over that of *any other child*, I revisit this mantra. I usually find my impulse has less to do with my children's well-being and more to do with my own fears or insecurities. The mantra *six of one* is a gentle reminder to bring awareness to my actions when interacting with other people's children—as much as with my own.

· No flaw is fatal ·

Sometimes radical acceptance of our children's limitations is extraordinarily difficult. Perhaps we can no longer see the radiance and magnificence in them. For those of us who have struggled in what seems to be a never-ending battle with a child over serious issues such as drugs, school failure, stealing, or aggression, things may seem hopeless. Our children are powerful forces. At times their emotional or behavioral problems seem to threaten the basic cohesion of our families. I have spoken to many loving, caring people who have admitted that they harbored deep feelings of anger and resentment toward their children. Of wanting them to just disappear. They longed to have someone else assume the burden of caring and raising their child. Not because they didn't love their child, but because they were exhausted. These feelings are extremely hard to admit as a parent. I have found the next two mantras to offer some relief to parents who are absolutely at the end of their rope. These mantras can help reframe the way you look at your child, but they are not curative. If your child or your family needs professional help to resolve serious issues, I urge you to find it. And use the mantras as a way to reclaim a more peaceful feeling toward your child as you get the help you need.

This is where Karen found herself. After years of trying to conceive, Karen decided to adopt two older children. She felt strongly about having more than one child, so she and her husband, Bob, requested a sibling pair. When the children arrived at their new home, the boy was seven and the girl was eleven. The social worker assigned to the children's case informed Karen and Bob that both children had experienced profound physical and verbal abuse. The young girl had also been molested by her uncle since the age of five.

The children had difficulty adjusting right from the start. They struggled in school, were rejected by peers, and did not seem to be attaching to Karen and Bob. Despite warnings from relatives, Karen and Bob decided to finalize the adoption. They felt they would be particularly suited to raising kids with emotional challenges because she was a social worker and he had done considerable volunteer work with at-risk youth. Karen noticed that she began having persistent negative feelings toward both children, but her daughter in particular. Despite her empathy for what her daughter had endured, she was embarrassed by her emotional outbursts and social skills deficits. When her daughter began displaying indiscriminant sexual behavior toward boys at school and toward Bob, Karen went over the edge.

The therapist that the family began seeing helped validate Bob and Karen's experience of having their lives upended. Unlike Karen had feared, the therapist didn't shame Karen about the enmity and resentment she felt toward her daughter. Eventually, however, she convinced Karen that in order to make the adoption successful, Karen was going to have to reframe the way she felt toward and interacted with her daughter. She did this by suggesting to Karen that many of the character traits and overt behaviors that her daughter exhibited weren't as *fatal* as she had made them out to be.

When Karen described to the therapist how her daughter embarrassed her in front of her colleagues by being overly dramatic and slightly vulgar about an incident at school, the therapist challenged her by asking, "So what?" When Karen relayed to the therapist that her daughter chewed with her mouth open, the therapist encouraged her to reinforce proper table manners. Then she said, "So is chewing with your mouth open enough to get you blacklisted? I mean, so what? Is it a *fatal flaw*?" Over time, Karen began to ignore her daughter's behaviors that had initially been most repugnant to her. At the same time she got help implementing solid behavior management interventions to improve her daughter's social skills and self-help abilities. Each time Karen repeated the mantra *no flaw is fatal*, it transformed her experience and softened her reaction to her daughter.

Every time I turn this question on an irksome quality that one of my kids exhibits, I am stunned by its power to defuse my judgment. Fixating on the flaw only serves to heighten its offensiveness. Often when faced with our children's rough edges, we run a negative or judgmental mantra in our head without being aware of what we are doing. Many times I've caught myself repeating over and over, "Oh man, this kid is so . . ."

One way of thinking about your child's aversive traits is to view them as being a spoonful of salt and his larger self or true nature as a big bucket of clean water. When you start to focus on a characteristic (lazy, irritable, hyperactive, inattentive) that annoys you, imagine yourself dropping the salt into the water. Were you to eat the salt alone it would be quite repulsive, much like an interaction with an ungrateful fourteen-year-old. But if you drank water from the bucket, not so bad. All of a sudden, the flaw *is not so fatal*. Still detectable, but not deadly. This practice allows us to see the deeper part of who our children are each time their foibles move to the fore of our attention. Let *no flaw is fatal* be a signal to focus on the essence of who your child really is, beneath the static of the annoyance. Each time the annoyance surfaces, greet it with a "no big deal attitude." Recognize your annoyance and imagine it dissolving like salt in water as you repeat the mantra.

Because this point is so crucial, it bears repeating—the mantra *no flaw is fatal* is not a substitute for finding professional intervention for our children's serious emotional or behavior problems such as with Karen's daughter's sexual behavior. Obviously, there are problems that require the type of help that is more complex. What the mantra can help us achieve is a more balanced and accepting day-to-day perspective on our child as he or she receives therapy or other types of assistance. Softening our view of our children and demonstrating positive regard has been shown repeatedly to improve their overall well-being. Let the mantra *no flaw is fatal* help put things into perspective.

· Open the door ·

According to the Dalai Lama, the practice of compassion is perhaps the single most effective way to instantly create a sense of tranquillity and inner peace—regardless of what is taking place around you. You may be thinking, "Hmmm, this sounds too good to be true." But wait, there's more! He states, "I think the practice of compassion is like a medication that restores serenity when one is very agitated . . . The great tranquilizer is compassion." This statement comes from a book entitled *Destructive Emotions—How Can We Overcome Them?* written by Daniel Goleman. The book documents a five-day summit between the Dalai Lama and a group of Western psychologists, neuroscientists, and philosophers. The overarching purpose of the collaboration was to examine the neuroscience associated with destructive impulses, cultural and biological factors related to affect, and Buddhist perspectives on strong negative emotions and techniques to transform them.

Throughout this conference the Dalai Lama continually pointed out the transformational power of compassion. He was also very clear that although manifesting a state of compassion is great for the world, the real hook is the enormous personal benefit it offers. The practice of compassion was put forth as the antidote for the most insidious and destructive emotions, including hatred, envy, and rage. There was even strong neurological evidence to support the fact that, over time, an ongoing practice of compassion can make lasting changes in one's brain structure. For mothers, anything that offers the possibility of instant serenity and tranquillity warrants a closer look. If it can transform hatred between warring nations (which the Dalai Lama offers evidence of), it can certainly change the way we feel toward a wayward child.

The conventional Buddhist definition of compassion is the wish that all beings become free from suffering and the root causes of suffering. Liberating people from suffering through enlightenment is one of the central goals of Buddhism. As mothers we know this urge well. We go to great lengths to protect our children from pain. Most mothers experience compassion for their children on an almost cellular level. It's in our gut. In fact, when Buddhist teachers attempt to evoke heightened states of compassion in their students, they often do so by using the example of a mother's unconditional love toward her child. Really, if you boil it down, an apt slogan for both Buddhists and mothers might be "Compassion Is Us." It's our business.

In keeping with this perspective, the mantra *open the door* serves as a reminder that at the heart of mothering is a vast reserve of tender compassion. At any time, we have the option to tap into that reservoir. When conjuring up compassion, it might be helpful to envision it as a soft but vibrant light that continually floats around the heart area. *Opening the door* allows the light to illuminate any difficult situation, causing us to literally see things differently. *Open the door* reminds us that no matter how distressed, disappointed, or frustrated we are with our child, there is a never-ending source of compassion available to us. The mantra urges us to bring forth the best in our mothering to deal effectively with our children. *It reframes our mission.* Basically, if you had to pick one mantra to get you through mothering, *open the door* would be a good contender. Compassion kindles good things. Compassion softens our reactions. It breeds patience and understanding. It helps dispel the negative (and often destructive) emotions that surface in response to our children's behavior.

What *open the door* doesn't mean is that we turn the other way when our children need discipline. It doesn't eliminate the importance of consequences. Embedded in the notion of compassion is that we act to eliminate future suffering. If a behavior-modification plan helps your child reduce negative behaviors, that is a far more compassionate response than just letting it slide.

Despite our love, concern, and compassion, there are times when we're less worried about our child's suffering and more worried about our own. If your young child is screaming in your ear or your teenager has used your house as an adolescent docking zone while you were away for the weekend, generating feelings of compassion for her might not be your first instinct. In fact, in the heat of the moment, it is more advisable to use the anger mantras. Last week, when my son spilled hot tea over my computer keyboard after I asked him at least four thousand times not to touch it, I knew that *open the door* wasn't the mantra for me. However, connecting to the mantra on an ongoing basis provides a broadened perspective and sane approach for dealing with tough situations.

As I watched my daughter and her friend standing by the dollhouse, I knew a showdown was brewing. "Give it to me now or else!" the guest suggested. "No way. I never ever want you to touch it!" was the retort. When the guest leaped forward and began throttling my daughter, I started in with the standard deescalation warning of *let's take a break and cool down*. However, before the words could leave my mouth, I saw my daughter pucker up and spit squarely on her aggressor's chest. I was horrified. My first impulse was to quarantine her. Looking closer at her reaction, however, I saw her bewilderment and confusion.

Although it was an unpleasant reaction on her part, it was a three-year-old's hasty attempt to find some way to protect herself and express her outrage. The mantra *open the door* allowed me to approach the situation (which involved a time-out for her) with a more open heart. *Open the door* helped neutralize my initially harsh and reactive impulses toward the situation so that I could respond more effectively.

Creating states of compassion toward our children can often be achieved more effectively if we spend some time engaging in the practice during times when we aren't under the gun. Take a moment and think of a time when you have felt compassion and loving kindness toward your child. Perhaps think of your child during a time when he has been vulnerable or in pain. Try to connect with your desire to free your child from this state of suffering. Seeing our children's errant behaviors through this prism of vulnerability can increase our compassion toward them. If you are having trouble creating a picture of compassion for your child at the present, see if imagining her as a younger child helps. Picture a hungry or tired infant. Cold or frightened. Keep searching until you discover a scenario that helps strengthen the feeling of compassion toward your child. Next time you feel upset or irritated by your child, see if revisiting this image instilled with compassion mitigates your negative feelings. Allow yourself to feel warmth, love, empathy, and compassion for your child, not just for his sake, but for your own as well.

· The less I feel it, the less I show it ·

I am not a good actress. When I am angry at my kids, they know it. And by and large, that's fine. It's good for kids to take stock of the fact that when they break their mother's prized rooster pitcher when playing basketball in the house, they may face a version of their mother that resembles Medusa more than June Cleaver. Seeing that their behavior elicits contingent responses from their caregivers is important. I do X, people feel Y, and then they do Z. And as long as our responses fall within the domain of healthy and appropriate behavior, all is well.

The problem occurs when we harbor long-standing negative beliefs about our children. In the 1960s, Robert Rosenthal, a researcher from Harvard, began looking at teachers' beliefs about their students' abilities and whether these expectations bore any effect on the children's performance in school. He found that teachers' beliefs (and their ensuing expectations) were powerful forces determining a teacher's treatment of the children and shaping how children saw themselves as learners. This was true even when teachers were convinced that they were concealing these attitudes. He labeled this dynamic the Pygmalion Effect. Later studies determined that even very young children are capable of reading subtle facial cues to determine whether teachers harbored critical or devaluing beliefs toward them. The term applied to the phenomenon of showing one's negative feelings without intending to "affect leakage."

Countless times my children have asked the question "Why are you looking at me like that?" "Like what?" I innocently reply. "Like *that*." On the occasions I've gone so far as to check out my face in the mirror, I see that my feelings have oozed over it—even when I thought my face was playing my cards close to the vest. Just as they do with their teachers, children pick up on our "negative affect leakage" as well. Here I am not talking about the times we express genuine feelings regarding our child's behavior. If you are angry, feel anger and, within reason, allow your child to see it. The danger lies when we hold on to residual negative feelings until they form stagnant judgments about who our child is. These judgments are then subtly transmitted when hot topics arise. This is where the mantra *the less I feel it, the less I show it* can help.

Julia is fifteen and lives in my apartment building. She is as charming and bright as a spring bird. She has the spirit of a vibrant yellow daffodil. However, in form Julia is very large. Still struggling to catch up with her recent growth spurt, at times she is ungainly. Her mother, on the other hand, was trained as a dancer. She makes getting the mail or sweeping look like a production for the New York City Ballet. Watching the pair of them can make even a stranger wince. Julia will inadvertently bump, smash, or uproot something, and her mother's face will drop whatever expression cloaked it and fall into a grimace. Onlookers get it, Julia gets it, everybody gets what her mom is feeling. Except her mom. She has no idea that this much information about her judgments regarding Julia's strange grace is washing over her face. But Julia's self-consciousness about her size and her constant apologizing about being accident prone is in large part traceable to the judgments reflected in her mother's eyes.

We all do this. It is virtually impossible not to have our fears, judgments, and disappointments about our children creep onto our faces. By and large, this is not a big deal. At the same time, chronic patterns of unspoken criticism can be hurtful to our children's sense of self. So how do we minimize the occurrence of negative affect leakage? What's a face to do?

The first step in reducing negative affect leakage requires us to take an honest look at what issues trigger our judgment, harsh criticism, and even disdain toward our children. What is it about your child that causes tension for you? After you've identified the behaviors or personality traits that elicit negative emotions, see if you can apply the previous mantras in this chapter. Take a minute and repeat to yourself that *no flaw is fatal*. Spend a moment and think of what's best in your child. Her fearlessness, her no-holds-barred honesty, her kindness or warmth. Then return to the quality in her that provokes your judgment. How does it compare to the greater part of who she is? How important is it really? Take a final moment and practice the mantra of *radical acceptance*.

If appropriate, allow yourself to see the flaw as an outgrowth of her strength—an element of her power that she must master before she has complete command of it.

At times I find myself seething over my daughter's unbreakable will. Today she insisted that I rebuckle her in the car three times until she was able to unstrap herself, jump down from the car, and close the door behind her. And of course, as we are doing this, we are growing exceedingly late for school. If she was unable to master even one step of the process, back to the drawing board. It took every ounce of my self-control, a few under-the-breath curses, and two mantras to get through the ordeal. My first instinct was to snatch her wildcat body and wrench her from the car. But then I saw that her single-mindedness is really just part and parcel of her deeply intrepid nature. She is a force to be reckoned with already, and although it is trying at times, it is equally impressive. Taking a moment to reframe her stubbornness took the mantra *no flaw is fatal* to another level. Not only is it not fatal, but it can reflect a wellspring of strength.

Once you have done your best to reframe your perspective of your child, it might help to take a deep breath in order to transmit this information to your body. Fez Answat, a meditation instructor I know, has a mantra I use often. *There is nothing as soothing as an exhalation.* And it's true. Try to visualize yourself breathing out your judgments. Do a quick scan of your body. Take inventory of your feelings. Then take a few letting-go breaths. When you're ready, look at your child again. *The less I feel it, the less I show it* means exactly that. You can't fake your face. If you feel resentment and disappointment, chances are it will show. But if you transform your judgments, even if you just take the edge off them, your affect will reflect that softening.

Chapter 8

· · ·

Change Happens

Just when we think we have our children figured out, they change. Not just things like tastes (love ham, hate ham), but elements of them that I considered immutable, like their temperaments. Aspects of them I thought would never change are suddenly poof. Of course some personality attributes stay constant across the lifespan. But many more things about our children, such as how they act and their shifting interests and desires, are up for grabs. In *The Tibetan Book of Living and Dying*, Buddhist teacher Sogyal

Rinpoche asks himself, "Why is it that everything changes?" The answer that comes back to him is always the same: "That is how life is." And that's how our children are—they are creatures that often defy prediction. Counting on virtually nothing *except* for change does two important things for me. It prevents me from being constantly blindsided by my children's continuous transformations, and it reminds me not to pigeonhole them to old versions of who they used to be.

· Anything's possible ·

Susan's oldest son, Peter, was hard to soothe as an infant and had considerable difficulty regulating his emotions. He disliked novelty and was very rigid in his preferences. Susan learned to accept Peter's disposition and was conscious to do what she could to help him cope with the world. She accepted this aspect of his personality with an open heart. Susan did a wonderful job helping him manage new situations more effectively and generally launching him into the world. By the time he was three, life was less of a struggle for him. But from the day he was born, Peter was a nervous, anxious child. As a baby he actually wore an expression of world-weariness. An old man came up to Susan once and said, "He's gonna be a poet, that one there. Deep, deep thoughts." At the age of six, Peter worried constantly about everything. Susan and her husband were extremely concerned about how he would take the news that they were moving to another city for his dad's new job.

Peter took it as expected—catastrophically. He screamed and cried from the moment Susan broke the news until the minute the moving truck arrived. He refused to accompany Susan to register at his new school. This step would be unnecessary, he explained, because *he wasn't going to school there—ever.* But he did go, and something happened to him there. A total shift came over him. He became more confident and easygoing. There was a lightness to his spirit that his parents had never observed before. Whereas before he clung to his mother in stores because "someone might try to steal me," now he seemed oblivious to harm. For the first time in his life he seemed happy. Same parents, same siblings, same extended family, but a very different outlook. When Susan called her mother and reported this radical change in Peter, her mother replied, "Well, *anything's possible.*"

Whether our kids change in dramatic or subtle ways, it requires us to modify the way we perceive them. We have to stop working from old scripts and outdated beliefs. The mantra *anything's possible* encourages us to expand our view of our children. By doing so, we are not only more attuned to them, but we send the message that we see what's going on for them. *We see them.*

We've all had the experience of interacting with someone locked into seeing the old version of who we are. It's like going through a time warp. Well, maybe I was a shy, introverted teen nerd who loved to spend hours doing macramé and listening to Anne Murray, but not so much anymore. It's like people are relating to a ghost of us, not who we are in the moment. The same is true for our children. Even our young children. And allowing obsolete notions of who they are to fade away is an essential part of seeing them as they evolve. The mantra *anything's possible* helps us do that.

· It comes out in the wash ·

We went to a Christmas party hosted by my mother's neighbors in Maine. The hosts have a thirteen-year-old daughter, Ginnie, who has clearly entered a new phase of her identity development. I remembered seeing Ginnie when she was small, riding her bike up and down the dirt road our houses shared. She was always a shy but radiant girl, with long blond braids and a sheet of freckles across her face.

When I first walked into their house, I did a double-take as I encountered a young woman who bore only a modest resemblance to the pigtailed girl. Ginnie's clothes were more like airy suggestions of pants and a shirt. Or sketched prototypes waiting for the material to be delivered and a seamstress to arrive. In order for her shirt not to slip from her body, she spent the better part of the party clutching the scrap of material to her collarbone until she disappeared into her bedroom with her friends. She had opted for the makeup look we termed "the raccoon" when I was a teenager, which consists of lots and lots of black mascara and eyeliner repeatedly applied until rings form above and below the lids. *Tres charmant* to you and your friends, torture to your mother.

Ginnie's mother, Claire, was earnestly trying to look and act accepting of her daughter and her friends, but it was clear that she may not have experienced 'coon eyes herself. Ginnie's mom was a lifelong academic and was a tenured professor of nine-teenth-century French literature at a nearby college. Claire had Ginnie and her younger brother when she was in her early for-ties. And while she was taking most of the teenage risk-taking behavior and experimentation in stride, some elements had stumped her. At one point in the evening, Claire leaned over to my mother and said, "I knew that they would go through changes and whatnot, but this is just, well, it just seems over the top. What should I do? You know, when I wash her clothes there's makeup all over her shirts and blouses." My mother looked softly at Claire and replied, "I know, but it washes out."

I think that my mom really meant—with no irony—that the mascara comes out in the wash, but her comment perfectly en-capsulated her laissez-faire attitude toward my sister's and my adolescent self-expression, even when those displays raised eyebrows. My sister's choice to move into an inner-city housing project for an extended stay with her best friend (no electricity) and my extremely electric blue hair were fine with her. "Oh, they're just *creative*." I don't think my mom needed a mantra like *it all comes out in the wash*, because her Buddha nature was shining through. I am often shocked when I look back at my adolescence and recall how my many anxiety-producing stages just rolled off her back with no judgment or fear on her part. She knew that the punk rock, the questionable boyfriends, the year off from college, would all *come out in the wash*. And they did.

But most of us will not take all of these new versions of our children in stride. Change is uncomfortable at times, not just for them, but for us, too. The mantra *it all comes out in the wash* is a reminder that teenagers are finding their voice and footing at some cost to our sense of peace and repose. We are consigned to worry. As long as they are safe and you maintain open communication about expectations regarding sex, drugs, alcohol, and their peer group, what's a little blue hair? The cost of holding on too tightly and resisting these forms of safe self-expression is usually far more dangerous than the rebellious act itself.

· No phase lasts forever ·

No matter who you are, there is most likely a phase of mothering that has or will rub you the wrong way. For my friend it's the obstinateness of the two-year-old. Some of the women on my hockey team are pulling their hair out over their teenage children's quest for freedom and battles over what they call the three C's: curfews, car keys, and college. For me it's feeling like a rhesus monkey with a newborn—the constant carrying and holding and nursing. It brings out my own adolescent desire for bodily freedom.

Rebecca couldn't stand the whining (though this will change after she practices the mantra *I can stand it* many, many, many times). Rebecca's first daughter, Jenny, entered that horrible stage that most children go through when much of what they say comes out in whinese. She found herself bristling each time she heard the shrill call of her child. The whining triggered Rebecca's irritation and stress from across the apartment, so that before she even started interacting with her daughter she felt that her patience was already taxed. It wasn't that Rebecca handled these situations badly or created a big drama in her head about how Jenny was whinier than other kids. But wondering how long the whining would go on increased her distress.

Rebecca's second daughter also became proficient in whinese at about the same age that Jenny had. But rooted in the back of her mind, Rebecca held the belief that the whining wasn't forever. This time she met her daughter's whining with the mantra *no phase lasts forever*. The biggest benefit of the mantra was the relief that Rebecca felt when she looked at her daughter's scrunched-up little face and knew in her gut that this wasn't forever. She did, however, attempt to hurry the phase along by rewarding nonwhiny behavior. Rebecca told her daughter that she didn't like her whining and would not answer her when she asked for things in whinese. (There were occasional, not completely mature acts of holding her hand to her ear and cocking her head as if to say, "Sorry, what was that? I can't make anything out *WHEN YOU WHINE LIKE THAT!*")

Regardless of how trying these periods are for us, they do pass. This mantra is not meant to encourage us to avoid what is going on in the moment. It isn't a call to tune out or check out from what our children's needs are, no matter how emotionally draining they might be. Instead, it is a reminder that while change sometimes brings strain and conflict, it also serves to unburden us from the developmental phases that are least pleasant. As you enter another battle with your three-year-old over why we need to bathe at least once a fortnight, know that *no phase lasts forever*. Take a deep breath and think forward to a time when you will be banging on the door, reminding her that two hours in the bathroom is ample preparation time for going to the movies. For many of us, the stress comes not only from the challenge of the phase, but from the unacknowledged belief that this phase will never end. Breathe deep and know that it will.

Chapter 9

. . .

Comparisons: The Good,
the Bad, and the Ugly

Toward the end of my first pregnancy, the obstetrician kept looking at me with glowing eyes, saying, "Oooh, it's gonna be a big one." And I remember feeling mild dread and timidly asking, "Does that type hurt more?" What triggered anxiety in me was actually just her attempt to instill a sense of pride in my offspring. Unbeknownst to me at the time, big babies are supposedly superior to small babies. But I caught on quickly. People would tell me I looked huge. "Oh yeah," I would say, nodding approvingly, "it's a whopper."

My second baby was very small and the pregnancy was the most anxiety-producing event of my life. As my delivery date neared, every two days I was hooked up to a monitor at the pre-natal high-risk unit of the hospital. They would take her anatomical measurements by sonogram and then somberly deliver the news. Compared to other babies in the eighth month of gestation, she was in the fifth percentile for height and weight. Everything else indicated a healthy baby. Toward the end of the pregnancy they would hospitalize me for hours—just to observe—even though my son would be stranded at a friend's house. This went on up until a week before my due date. Finally, I was reduced to tears. On that day I had a new doctor who looked at the baby's vital signs, noticed my wrecked nerves, and unhooked the monitoring belt. He then surveyed the mass of sonogram technicians, nurses, and residents and said, "Look at the mother—she is five feet tall. How big did you expect the baby to be?" He then ordered me not to come back until I was in labor. And I didn't.

Comparisons are part of life. We are social creatures who are powerfully influenced by those around us. We learn by watching others, imitating them, and appraising our performance compared to them. Being adept at observing others and altering our behavior can be highly adaptive, as when we attempt to acculturate to new environments or master novel tasks. Albert Bandura, a prominent social psychologist, pointed out that most of what we learn in life is accomplished simply by watching others. In many ways, making discernments, judgments, and comparisons are highly adaptive tendencies. Comparisons can let us know if we're on the right track.

In terms of mothering, most of us aren't always sure of what's normal and appropriate development when we get our first baby. So we look around at the other babies to see if ours is eating, crawling, sleeping, crying, burping, and pooping the way she should. Sometimes these comparisons can help our children. Betsy noticed that her daughter was lagging behind other children verbally in her play group. She asked her doctor's advice and he recommended that she consult with a speech therapist. After sixteen months of early intervention, she was talking up a storm. As mothers of teenagers, we look to see what responsibilities, freedoms, and privileges other kids are allowed to give us a sense of whether we're in the ballpark with our expectations. This may ratify our suspicions that not all sixteen-year-olds in your daughter's class have a one A.M. curfew, despite her attestations.

Making comparisons can also help normalize our feelings about our children's behavior. They can put to rest suspicions that there is a train wreck headed our way. I was at the park listening to a woman tell her friend how resistant her son was to being potty trained. She said, "He's three and a half. I don't know what to do. I read every book ever written and still he won't get near the toilet. He's going to college in diapers. I know it." The other woman just looked, said, "My son," and held up four fingers. The first woman replied in surprise, "Really? Hmm." A look of relief spread over her face.

I have found this to be true countless times. When I have a genuine fear or anxiety about my children, I go to the people I trust. Compassionate peers. And then I tell them what is happening and ask whether red flags are going up for them. Nine times out of ten, my fears are allayed. And on the tenth time, when they see a real problem, they tell me. You don't need a bevy of these people. One will do. These kind of checking-in friends use comparisons to increase your sense of safety and well-being, not the opposite.

WHEN COMPARISONS TURN TOXIC

The downside of comparisons is that they can increase our stress and our dissatisfaction with our children and ourselves. Comparisons sometimes hinder us from listening to our instincts. They can block us from fully seeing and appreciating our children. Debra was very proud of her son's improvement in reading until she went to talk to his teacher and found out he was in the lowest reading level in the class. It took her some time and a few reinforcing mantras to reframe his success in terms of his own progress. Once she was able to do that, she felt more appreciative and moved by his accomplishment and the tremendous effort it required of him. In our competitive, achievement-frenzied society, we can often get locked into appraising ourselves and our children by looking outward rather than inward.

· Narrow your focus ·

I put dinner on the table and immediately the baby hurled his plate across the table for his brother to catch, which he did not. My daughter curled up in a fetal position on the floor and expressed her deep disdain for vegetables, and meat, and dairy products. My son lay down on the window bench where the kids usually sit so that only his feet were visible as I scanned the kitchen. I took a deep breath, sized up the situation, and *narrowed my focus.*

Narrowing your focus is an explicit call not to summon the image of a child who you secretly believe to perform in a superior fashion to your own child (or in this case, all of your children) and let the comparisons begin! The danger of comparisons is insidious whether you make them in your head or, worse yet, share them with your errant children. The end result is always the same. Comparisons intensify your anger at your child, make your child resent you, and plant the seeds of inferiority, competition, and general unrest for all involved.

On previous occasions, I had increased my stress and resentment often brought about by dinner by comparing my children to the Dailey children, whose interest in food is legendary. (Our babysitter recently admired our youngest child's diverse palate, but then qualified her statement by saying, "I mean he's a good eater, but he's no Jack Dailey.") Daileys sit down and devour entire fowl. Jack could polish off an entire meatloaf by himself at the age of six. And Daileys love food so much that warnings about being ejected from the table if they don't get up off the floor this instant are unheard of. The Daileys always look at my children with chagrin and bemusement, wondering why they are so willing to put a perfectly good meal in jeopardy. Daileys do not enjoy eating at my house, because the antics of my children at dinner create an unpleasant distraction from their dining pleasure.

But this time I didn't conjure up the Daileys. Mostly because what happens when I do is predictable and very unpleasant for me. The difference between my children's behavior and the Daileys' incites me. Then I blame myself: "Where did I go wrong? This is all my fault. If only I'd been more disciplined about dining. Now I've made dinner such a battle, it's squelched any inborn inclination to eat." Then I get very, very angry at my children. More than my children's actual antics, it's the comparison that increases my displeasure and frustration. So this time, instead of opening my range of vision to include the Daileys, I stuck to my own kids. I held each of them responsible for their own poor behavior, expressed my expectations for proper dining etiquette (feet *off* table), then meted out consequences. I *narrowed my focus* away from the Daileys and all the appreciative well-mannered children across the globe and settled my gaze on the children in front of me. It helped.

• Bubble-wrapped •

When I was in fifth grade there was a movie in which John Travolta played the role of a boy who had no immune system or some other serious medical malady. I don't think the illness was as important as the treatment method. The solution was to place him in a plastic bubble so that no pathogens could invade his environment and threaten his failing white blood cells. The image was always quite alluring to me, and many times during my childhood I yearned to be placed in such a hermetically sealed vault.

We know from experience that there are children who need to be *bubble-wrapped* more than others—protected from the world. Buffered from unkindness. As unfair and sinister as it seems, the world treats children of different temperaments in quite discrepant ways. The world loves an easygoing, hard-to-ruffle baby. The world does not so readily embrace the screaming, hard-to-soothe, shrieks-upon-seeing-your-face type. Not only does this type of personality discrimination seem blatantly wrong; it seems counterproductive. How's a kid supposed to learn to become happy and self-regulated if people reject the few ways he has to express himself? And I've seen these response patterns from people expected to *know* better.

When Adele had her first baby, he was, as they say where I come from, "a real wet cat." He appeared as though someone had attempted—and halfway succeeded—to pickle him. His face was always screwed up in some display of discomfort. He squirmed when anyone tried to hold him, including his mother. He projected the sense that he had gotten off the bus at the wrong stop and was desperately trying to remedy his error. He just didn't seem happy to be here. Adele saw the uncharitable way that people beheld Frank, and she didn't like it one bit. She heard every comment imaginable: "Oh, it must be so hard to have a baby like that. How do you manage?" "Is there something wrong with him?" "So who does he take after, you or your husband?"

So Adele came up with a highly effective visualization that she invoked anytime Frank interacted with someone. Adele imagined that a bright light surrounded Frank and that this buffer protected him from all intentional or accidental caustic influences. In her mind, she imagined that every look or comment that got through the light shield had been transformed into love before it impacted him.

Whether this benefited Frank directly is debatable. But it helped him indirectly in that it soothed and relaxed Adele and reframed the way she perceived her son in the world. She felt less anxious and troubled by his personality. Her feelings of overprotectiveness decreased, and she became more supportive of his exploratory behavior. This, in turn, helped Frank achieve a sense of mastery and competence in his world. As he ventured outward, he focused less on his uncomfortable, irritable feelings. Frank became more content. And each time a subtle barb or downright offensive comparison was made about Frank, she saw it dissolved by the light that surrounded her baby. Essentially, she *bubble-wrapped* him (or really herself) from the world to minimize any damages that might befall him on his journey.

We can't control how the world perceives our babies or young children. Over time, we can teach them that there are certain behaviors that will create acceptance and those that will usually draw rejection. We then have to guide them in determining how much importance to place on the world's view of them. We must help them sort through how much to prize external validation and whether, at times, this should be ignored for one's internal convictions. As they grow, we can inoculate them when necessary from the world's opinions and judgments. But for infants and toddlers, the qualities that precipitate various reactions from the world are largely biologically determined in the form of temperament. And in this case, it is the mother who needs inoculating from the world.

When people draw unkind comparisons about your baby or child, softly repeat the mantra *he's bubble-wrapped* or *he's surrounded by light*. Imagine the pointed comparison or subtle criticism falling on the ground after bouncing harmlessly off the baby. Each time a comparison or negative comment is directed toward your child, use it as a reminder to spend a moment with him in love, affection, kindness, and acceptance. You protect the baby by your love, and the mantra protects you with its image of immunity and safety.

Chapter 10

. . .

The Bounce-Back Factor

I was seven months pregnant with my third child. (I like to start
each story that involves me being in dereliction of duty with the
preface that I was pregnant or nursing or recovering from some
aspect of children. It's gentler lighting.) I had just been to a doctor's visit alone and I decided to treat myself to a "fancy" lunch,
which involves eating a meal in the seated position that I ordered
intentionally for me. I looked lovingly at my soup. I felt the
warm glow of not having to forcibly hold a child in a bench seat

while dropping pieces of pizza in her mouth like a weary pigeon feeding her young. However, as I let my defenses down, it slowly crept into my awareness that there were an awful lot of school-age children loose on New York City streets for lunchtime on a Wednesday.

I shook it off as a private school phenomenon until I heard the little girl next to me ask why she didn't get to eat lunch at school. Then I listened with growing interest as the mother explained that all the schools in New York were dismissed early. Eventually, the picture erupted on my pregnant, walnut-sized brain and I panicked. Waddling to the closest pay phone, I learned that I did not have the school's number. Finally, I called my friend (my organized, marks-the-half-days-on-a-calendar friend) and asked her to pick up my son. He waited for two character-building hours.

As I was driving home to retrieve him, the voice of one of my first clinical psychology professors intruded gently into my thoughts. During his lectures he would systematically lay out an array of grave childhood psychological disorders and their putative origins (read: parents caused this). Just as he could see that we were drawing the conclusion that there's no getting out of childhood unscathed, he would pat his notes and say, "but they're *born to bounce back*." Along the same lines, I had another professor who was convinced that babies needed the stress of birthing to activate certain functions in the brain and body. She likened it to crocuses forcing their way up in the snow. That appealed to me greatly on face value—not only are we humans born to withstand hardship, but it heightens our functioning. We are resilient by nature.

• They're tough •

We all know this instinctively. We learn from challenge, hardship, and disappointment. We see what we are made of and are strengthened by hurdling (or plowing through) another obstacle. As crazy as it sounds, my sister's falling off the monkey bars and fracturing her arm in two places improved my self-esteem as a youngster inordinately. We were alone in the playground. I looked at the bone protruding from her arm, sized up the situation, ran two miles uphill, tracked my mother down, and led her to the park. I then found a stranger to help drive the car while my mother held my sister in the back seat. I was a hero. It was stressful, but good for developing a sense of competence and self-reliance.

So why do we feel guilty every time we let our kids down? Why do we berate ourselves and feel like heels? Because that's what good, attentive, trying-to-do-better mothers do. They are on a never-ending mission to safeguard their children from harm. And this is an evolutionarily sound instinct. But the mantra *they're tough* is not just a way to soften our guilt; it is a reminder that unpleasant things can sometimes strengthen our kids and tap previously unknown resources. In fact, when we attempt to insulate our children entirely from disappointment, anxiety, and fear, we deprive our kids of the opportunity to learn to cope with these feelings in a loving, secure environment. If they're going to face these feelings sooner or later, we might as well equip them to handle them safely and constructively.

Back to my son (I may have forgotten him in real life, but not the story). As I opened the door to my friend's house, I saw my six-year-old on the floor playing busily. He looked up and smiled at me. Anne told me that he had been crying when she picked him up, but recovered quickly. Later that night he told me how scared he felt and worried that he might have to sleep at school in the classroom. I listened and apologized, felt like a jerk, promised to *always* read the notes his teacher sent home, and praised his bravery. I also told him how lucky we are that even when his mom screws up we have people in our lives ready to help him and keep him safe. I told him that now he'd done the hard part. If I ever forgot him again or was late for some reason, he would know in his heart that nothing really bad would happen. He stopped what he was doing and said, "So when are you going to forget me next?" So much for the halo effect. I told him I didn't really know, and that I wasn't *planning* on it, but if I did he'd be ready. He agreed.

• They will forgive •

Martha had not been at her finest that morning. For months she had been dealing with her mother's cancer—physically helping her through radiation and chemotherapy, taking care of her father as her mother recovered, and dealing with the bureaucracy of insurance and hospitals. The stress of traveling back and forth from Boston to Washington, D.C., was getting to her. Martha hurried to get her kids ready for school. Lunches were strewn across the counter, homework was still not complete, and her four-year-old daughter refused to get dressed. As the tension mounted, Martha began thinking that she had to leave again this weekend to fly back down to her parents. She looked around at her house, which was in total shambles, and felt herself start to buzz with stress.

She called for her daughter to come and eat her breakfast. And when she appeared, she was completely naked, having stripped herself out of the clothes that Martha had patiently cajoled her into. Martha looked at the child's naked little body and snapped. She grabbed the little silverfish by the wrist and began jamming her shirt over her head, screaming all the while, *This is not helpful behavior to take your clothes off that Mommy put on you when you know that we are getting into the car in just a few seconds why did you do that I can't believe you did that!* All punctuated by grunts. It was like dressing an uncooperative rag doll, her little doll arms flailing about. Shortly, everyone was crying. Martha stepped aside and let her husband finish the dressing. As they were driving somberly to school a while later, Martha reminded herself that over and over again her children have shown their willingness to forgive. She told her daughter that she was very sorry that she treated her so roughly. She explained that although it was no excuse, she had been very tired lately and upset because of Grandma's sickness. Martha asked her daughter if she could forgive her. Her daughter let out an exasperated sigh and said with incredulity, "Ughhh, of course I do, you're my mommy."

In the chapter on the core Self, the concept of self-forgiveness and the accompanying mantras are explored at length. Further on in this chapter, the notion of forgiving our children is addressed. But in terms of thinking of our children's predisposition toward resilience and health, it is important not to overlook their innate capacity for forgiveness. From an early age, teaching our children the language of forgiveness is a powerful tool in resolving the emotional conflicts that occur in our families almost daily. I get sick of hearing my own voice saying "sorry," but I know it's important to do when I've been careless or hurtful. When teaching forgiveness to our children, we clarify that in forgiving, we aren't condoning or excusing the negative or hurtful *act*. We are instead forgiving the person. When we ask their forgiveness, it is essential that we are clear that our harmful behavior—no matter how explainable because of our stress—is not acceptable. And before we can ask for their forgiveness, we must offer a genuine apology. This apology must clearly separate what we've done from who we are. Kids get this. I've seen even young children be able to distinguish between being and behavior. My three-year-old often says to us, "Even when I make bad choices, you still love the me part, right?"

The mantra *they will forgive* can be restorative, especially when we have really messed up. I have worked with parents who, because of their own deeply rooted psychological problems, have done terrible things to their children. They have abused them, abandoned and neglected them, taken advantage of their intrinsic trust, and lied over and over to them. These parents often withdraw from their children with the belief that "there's no way this kid will forgive me after what I've done." In fact, the opposite is true—children are willing to forgive at almost any cost. I have watched these same children, some still reeling from the trauma, try to find a way to emotionally reconnect with their parents. Often these children require time and space to acknowledge and accept their anger over their parents' offenses and to understand their parents' emotional limitations. Often it's not psychologically healthy or advisable for them to be in their parents' presence.

But the urge to be emotionally and physically reconnected with their parents is as powerful as a tidal pull. So just when you think your children won't forgive you for your transgressions, no matter how harshly you judge yourself, think again. Every time you feel as though you have let your child down, failed him, or hurt her, repeat the mantra *they will forgive*. Being aware of our children's forgiving nature is essential as a reminder to respect and protect this quality in them and to appreciate its ability to heal the harm our actions have caused.

· Pain is part of it ·

We all watched with tension as the four boys stood in a group deciding what to play at the park that day. We didn't really care *what* they played so much as *how* they played it. Although the boys had been friends for years (they were now five), recently they had started to shun one particular member of the group, Jon. They teased him, rejected him, called him names, ignored his attempts to join games. (If it sounds a lot like a modern version of "Rudolph the Red-Nosed Reindeer," it's because it *was* a lot like Rudolph.) And the apparent motivation was simple: because they could. Jon was a good target, since he is the most sensitive one of the bunch and an earnest, sweet, easy-to-read kid. It was horrific and reminded me why I never finished the book *Lord of the Flies*. My friends looked at me and said, "You're a psychologist. Is this normal?" It may have been normal, but it wasn't good.

The group of mothers descended on the boys, issuing reprimands, explaining empathy, and following up with consequences. But the more they intervened, the worse the group tormented Jon. After a few weeks of trying to make it work, it became clear that these interactions were damaging to the child. Jon felt powerless, extremely distressed, and began expressing distorted negative beliefs about himself. He blamed himself for his rejection, though from our more removed perspective, he was just the unlucky recipient of social aggression. One on one, the boys did fine, but in a pack it brought out the worst in them. It was like watching wolves. They all looked to the alpha boy for their lead. If he said lunge, they did. None of the other kids was eager to take Jon's place. Finally, Jon's mom said enough was enough. She put a moratorium on group playdates.

At home, Jon spent a great deal of time thinking about what had happened. He tried to extract meaning from his friends' behavior. His mother listened to his fears and sadness, but each time he looked inward to rationalize their treatment of him, she turned it back on the aggressors. Although watching her son being tormented was extremely difficult for her, she didn't avoid the subject. Instead, she used the experience to start a dialogue about why people bully, their feelings of inadequacy, and the fact that they don't always know better ways to manage their problems. And each time she felt herself getting lost in her own feelings of anger toward the other boys (and sometimes their mothers), she reminded herself that in terms of growing up, *pain is part of it*. In fact, one of the four noble truths of Buddhism is the explicit acknowledgment that suffering is part of the human condition.

As time went on, Jon developed friendships outside of this peer group. These connections increased his sense of social competence and made him feel less dependent on that group. As painful as the experience had been for Jon, he had learned a tremendous amount. A social-worker friend his mother knew taught him some techniques to minimize the likelihood of being bullied. As his confidence grew, he asserted himself more in the face of aggression, which reduced the bullying behavior because the bullies weren't being reinforced by Jon's submissive reaction. Although the process had been difficult, Jon admitted to his mother two years later that he learned a lot from the experience.

From our own childhoods, we know that there is unpleasantness involved in growing up—*pain is part of it*. The purpose of this mantra is twofold. The first point of the mantra is a reminder that *everybody* suffers. Sometimes we develop tunnel vision in relation to our children or life experiences. It's the whole "why me?" anti-mantra. A small voice in us calls out that we (or our children) are somehow experiencing more suffering or hardships than others. But the mantra *pain is part of it* reminds us that it's nothing personal. Childhood holds its fair share of tribulations and difficulties. It's part of the deal. We are no more able to sanitize our children's world and protect them from pain than we are to breathe for them. And we wouldn't want to. As hard as they are to watch (so, so hard to watch), these trials are part of what makes kids grow into wiser, more mature individuals.

The second purpose of the mantra *pain is part of it* is to do as Jon's mother did—face our discomfort regarding our children's suffering and be present and available for them. It's natural to want to avoid pain, but using this mantra may help you step back into the ring when you are most needed. Of course there are times when our children, especially our teenagers, want to lick their wounds in private or in the company of their friends. Our part is not to force our support on them but to make sure that it's available. The more we fight the pain that emerges in our lives, the more offensive and unbearable it seems. When I find myself overly resisting the presence of pain or discomfort in my children's lives, I know it's time for this mantra.

· This will heal ·

As I mentioned earlier, my friend Penny is a pediatrician, so she is in the unfortunate position of being called by all of her friends every time our children have fevers, hits to the head, massive bleeding, and other bizarre or life-threatening ailments. We have a running joke about her medical advice, though. While she always listens patiently to our list of complicated symptoms, her response rarely varies: "Yeah, that'll heal. Got any ice?" Once she came over when one of my kids had a fever of 106 degrees. She looked compassionately at him, stroked his face, and said, "Yeah, got any Tylenol?" I looked suspiciously at her. "Shouldn't I take him to the hospital or something?" "Nah, what's the point?" she said reassuringly. At first I thought she was nuts. I went so far as to question whether she actually attended medical school (she did). But after years of friendship, I see that she's right. Nine times out of ten, it just heals. Lest I misrepresent her skills and beliefs, she does snap shoulders back into place, set broken bones, administer antibiotics, and stitch kids up. But she also respects the body's natural tendency to heal itself.

Each time I see blood streaming down one of my children's faces or watch anxiously as a cough worsens, I repeat the mantra *this will heal* before I allow myself to entertain one more thought. Practicing this mantra sets the stage for the rest of my reactions to unfold. In psychology there is the notion of a holding environment. Basically, it means a safe and nurturing space from which to operate. Saying the mantra, no matter what, *this will heal*, creates a holding environment for me to begin attending to my child's sickness or accident. I take a deep breath, repeat the mantra, expect the worst, hope for the best, and survey the damage. Allowing myself this pause is my cue not to plunge down the cascading waterfall inside the barrel. Instead, the mantra is a reminder to become a more dispassionate observer. I watch the barrel hurl itself over the cliff, but I'm not in it. Instead of getting caught up in the drama of the accident, I'm available to help in whatever way I can.

The same is true for emotional injuries. By and large, they will heal. John Bowlby was a psychiatrist whose work was responsible for the creation of attachment theory. One of his beliefs is that mothers who are attuned to their children act as a secure base. Safe and securely attached children then feel competent to explore their environments. They are less anxious, fearful, and mistrustful of their world because they have internalized the belief that they are fundamentally safe and protected. Securely attached children anticipate that the people they meet will be kind and treat them with respect because that's what their experience with their primary caregiver has taught them. When, instead, they are hurt by others or experience failure, most are able to treat it as a stumbling block and move on. When our children know they are loved, when they experience consistency from their caregivers, they have a natural inclination to heal. Actually, we all have an innate drive to be well. But those children who have caring, supportive caregivers are a step ahead of the game in terms of emotional recovery. It's heart-wrenching to see our children let down, treated disrespectfully by others, or have their trust broken. Yet at the same time, we can breathe with some relief knowing they come fully equipped to heal.

Of course, not everything heals—we know that. Terrible

sicknesses and tragedies befall children. And at times, the gravity of those illnesses is too much to withstand. If you have lost a child to illness or an accident, my deepest and most sincere sympathy goes out to you. I am not sure if there is any greater source of pain or sorrow than the death of a child. Raising other children in the wake of a loss of this magnitude requires great strength and fortitude. If your children have experienced the death of a sibling, I hope that the mantra *this will heal* offers some degree of solace and comfort while attending to your child's grief and loss. Many schools, community centers, and hospitals offer sibling grief groups, which may help normalize some of the feelings your child might be experiencing after the death of a sibling. Watching small steps in our child's healing process reinforces our own belief in the mantra *this will heal*. With enough practice and trust, a self-fulfilling prophecy evolves.

There are other situations in which our children do not seem to be recovering or are making slow progress. If you have adopted a child with serious emotional or behavioral problems or have a child with a serious mental illness, the journey toward health may seem undetectable. However, within even the children whose conditions seem most recalcitrant, there is the push to heal. Some of my clients have been through emotional tragedies that seem almost impossible to heal from, such as rape, losing their parents or siblings to violence, or being the victim of chronic abuse and neglect. Most of these children have not benefited from a secure and loving base from which to develop. Yet repeatedly I have watched many, if not the overwhelming majority, heal, given enough time, love, support, and safety.

When using this mantra, there are some things you can do to help deal with the feelings that arise when we see our child is suffering. As you look at your child in pain—either emotional or physical—notice what feelings arise in you. To the best of your ability, allow them to surface and attempt to identify them. Observe your fear, anxiety, dread, sadness, and panic just as they are. Acknowledge that these feelings are a signal to activate a helpful, protective, loving response. Before acting on any one feeling, just see what comes up without doing anything.

A feeling that often arises in me when my children get hurt is anger. I find myself scolding them for tipping back in their chair after I warned them a *million* times. Then I see that under my anger is frustration at being unheeded. And under my frustration is fear that they might get seriously hurt. I am not always successful, but when I approach each new calamity with the mantra *it will heal*, I allow myself the time to let these feelings surface, be acknowledged, and pass by like a darting school of fish. That leaves me free to respond to my child's pain without getting stuck in my initial knee-jerk reactions. I find that in doing this, I'm more effective in comforting my child and myself.

Chapter 11

. . .

Forgiving Our Kids

Being a mother is just code for being in the forgiveness business. On a daily basis, our children act in ways that require us to forgive them. Siblings harm siblings, we are purposely ignored or disrespected, rules are broken, property is damaged, and we are put into awkward and unpleasant situations on their behalf. Sometimes there are periods when we lose touch with the loving, wise, and peaceful nature of our child. Being a mother is a call to forgive continually. In fact, the spirit of mindful mothering is really just one of ongoing forgiveness. It is a choice we make over and over again to see our children with compassion and understanding. In fact, the groundwork of forgiveness can be laid by using the compassion mantra *open the door.*

Without forgiveness, we risk carrying around our resentment, anger, and frustration. We risk getting lost in the fog of our residual emotion. When we think of forgiving our children, most likely specific events or disruptive behaviors are the ones we most readily identify as requiring our forgiveness. Once a mother came to a workshop wanting help in forgiving her son for pushing her other son off the top of a toolshed (he was fine, but we're not sure why they were up there) in a moment of sibling anger. She was furious with her child and needed serious guidance and support in forgiving him. Everyone in the workshop agreed that dislodging your brother from a shed qualified as an act in need of forgiveness.

However, there are other circumstances or personal qualities that creep in and cause negative feelings toward our children—less obvious ones. How often do we think it necessary to forgive our children for being sick, disabled, difficult, thirteen, needy, angry, clingy, disruptive, fearful, loud, or any other quality that makes it hard on us? Sometimes we are not fully aware that certain characteristics are contributing to the undercurrent of judgment and hostility we feel toward our child. When I find myself saying or thinking while in conflict with my child, "You are always so . . ." or "You never . . . ," then I know I need to work on forgiveness. At these times I have become fixated on one particular quality at the risk of missing the bigger, deeper nature of my child. When I find myself lost in the wish that they could be other than they are, I look to forgiveness.

In earlier sections of this book, I have discussed the fundamental elements and purpose of forgiveness, so I won't repeat myself here. But I will stress again that forgiveness is not about forgiving negative acts; it is about forgiving the child who acted out of fear, confusion, impulsivity, or neediness. The mother who forgave her son for pushing his brother off the barn roof was not forgiving the shove. She was forgiving her child. She was seeing beyond his behavior into the essential nature of her child—one of undiluted goodness.

What follows is a three-pack of forgiveness mantras. The first mantra is designed to release the feelings of anger or resentment you might be feeling toward your child. The second mantra is a call to connect to your child's true nature or lightness, regardless of his behaviors. The third is a reminder to create a new vision of your child each day—one full of limitless potential and boundless joy.

· Whack the piñata ·

Louisa's middle son, Charles, had struggled in school most of his life. He'd been diagnosed with attention-deficit/hyperactivity disorder in kindergarten and had learning difficulties as well. Louisa was accustomed to the calls from teachers complaining that Charles was off-task, impulsive, sloppy, behind in his work, and sometimes disruptive. She had also grown used to the tight smiles on the faces of parents when she picked him up after play-dates. Although Louisa and her husband handled the stress fairly well, at times she would get stuck feeling very negatively toward her son. One day she said, "You know, each time he messes up or does something that makes me cringe, it's like getting a speeding ticket. And I keep shoving them into the glove compartment without really dealing with them. I know they're there and they really bother me, but I just keep driving around. I feel tense and nervous, like every teacher or mother or kid in the park is another person who's gonna give me a ticket. The worst thing is that I hold it against him even though I know he can't help it. I'm afraid someday I'm really going to snap on him."

We've all been in a similar situation. Little (or big) annoyances build up and at some point we blow. We reel off a complete list of every rule they've infracted since we started keeping score. These diatribes often include phrases like "while we're on the subject" and "speaking of which." We don't want to feel so angry at our child, but we really, really do. The best mantra I've heard to start the process of forgiveness comes from a psychologist friend who translated a therapy exercise she uses with clients into the mantra *whack the piñata*. When she finds herself at the end of her rope with one of her own kids, she visualizes all of his or her transgressions written out in detail on pieces of paper. Then each one gets put inside a giant piñata. (You are free to select any animal or cartoon form. Do not visualize the head of your own child.) Next, she visualizes herself standing, feet firmly planted, smashing the piñata to smithereens. With the last whack, the pieces of paper explode from the piñata and are swept away by a strong wind.

I have used this mantra on many occasions when I feel ever-increasing pressure in the bottle and my cork is about to blow. Typically, an alarm sounds in my head and I know I need to release the mounting tension. *Whack the piñata* helps me transform myself into a more objective observer. It is a call to shift the way I am experiencing my child—no matter what he's doing. *Whack the piñata* is a reminder that we have the power to release our anger by *choosing* to let it go. Sometimes we have to sit with our anger for a while—and that's fine. At some point, however, we will most likely find that we want to be released. Or perhaps we realize that by not surrendering our anger, we're constrained to act and think in certain ways. Other times we may recognize that not releasing our anger presents a real threat to our children—especially if we're at our boiling point.

Whack the piñata is a particularly useful mantra when patterns of irritating behavior are building a strong case against your child. To make this mantra really effective, try to identify every single infuriating behavior (tantrum at the store, tantrum at bed, tantrum at dinner, pushing sister/brother, refusing to do homework) contributing to your negative feelings. Picture yourself putting them in the piñata. And then see yourself whack, whack, *whacking away at the piñata* until the papers clear and every last one is swept away.

· See the light ·

Whack the piñata is a mantra meant to clear the air. The first steps of forgiveness are identifying and processing the feelings of annoyance, frustration, and anger that we are holding on to. This mantra helps us to clear away some of the smoke clouding us from seeing and relating to our child in a more neutral or objective manner. Our children will constantly make us angry for things both in and out of their control. Sometimes just the fact that they are children (and at times are noisy, messy, inconsiderate, forgetful, and needy) can make us angry and resentful. We look at a clean house and see it single-handedly destroyed five minutes after the school bus arrives. People are hungry and tired, but rather than request food or a drink, they bleat like possessed goats. Our rational minds know that these are behaviors that all children demonstrate. But our subjective, tired-of-cleaning-up minds are ready to snap at the children we have labeled as careless, selfish, and unreasonable—ours.

But once the air is clear, what next? In her book *Forgiveness: A Bold Choice for a Peaceful Heart*, Robin Casarjian defines forgiveness as a "decision to see a pure essence, unconditioned by personal history, that has limitless potential and is always worthy of respect and love." Letting go of our anger doesn't mean that we will automatically see our child in this way. Seeing the true nature of our child—his or her core goodness—is a choice we make. *It is a way of looking rather than sitting back and being shown.* Our children might show us all kinds of unpleasantries, but forgiveness is a decision not to be fooled or put off track. Instead we look beyond fear, insecurities, and frustration and see our child's true nature, his innate power, lovableness, and promise.

◦ Wipe the slate clean ◦

There are those days. Mine happen a lot in the summer, when there is no school and there are long, long hours of unstructured time. During these days, there are endless opportunities for things to devolve. Well-intentioned trips to the beach or museum with three children under the age of seven can lead the best of us down the river. And it is not your imagination that the days are longer in the summer, leaving you to ponder, "Why does the sun stay up so long in July? Why?" For some reason, summer is the time that things brew in our family, rising to the top and begging to be skimmed off in order to clarify the broth.

There are nights when I use every mantra written in this book and still find my ears ringing at the end of the day. I stumble to bed and ask, "Did that really happen?" More important, "Will it happen again?" I am hard pressed to identify one thing in particular. But for the sake of the mantra, let's assume that I am sent overboard by the constant whining because people are bored and want to watch TV (no), eat chips at 8:30 A.M. (no), use a rope to ride the dog (no), go to the water park even though Dad went to work on Saturday (no, no, no). At these times it is very easy to create a story about what my kids are like—whiny, impatient, demanding, self-centered, dependent, and unimaginative (except for the part about the dog). I am tired of them and they are most certainly tired of me.

What doesn't help at this point is turning up the heat under the pot by stoking the flames of my annoyance and disappointment. What does help is the mantra *wipe the slate clean*. After they have gone to bed and we have been separated by at least two hours of sleep-filled noncontact, I make my rounds. I go into each of their rooms and look at them sleeping peacefully. (Every parenting book I have ever read includes this technique, because it *really* does work.) As I watch them breathing, I let go of the day. I release my judgments. By *wiping the slate clean,* I undo the prediction that tomorrow will be just as bad or that they will act the same way. I unlace the straitjacket I have clasped them in with the story of how they are always this way or that. I see a thousand possibilities instead of one. I am reawakened to their divine nature. By practicing forgiveness each night, I release us all from the hamster wheel we sometimes get stuck on. By choosing to forgive, I find them again and again.

Part Three

Mantras for
Our Mothers
(and Some for the Others)

As I do a long visual sweep of the Thanksgiving bounty about to be placed on the table, my heart swells with love and warmth. People have traveled from far and wide to come together and revel in family bonding. Parents, siblings, and friends are good-naturedly crammed along the perimeter of two makeshift tables. My husband has cooked enough for an army. I have cleaned and gone so far as to dig out napkins made of cloth rather than folded-up bits of paper towel. We are parents. These are our children. Here is our family.

Within seconds after the blessing, two of my children have left the table because they "hate turkey anyways. And I don't care what you say, it does *not* taste just like chicken." Our parents assume "here we go again" faces, which puts us in the position of leaving the table to retrieve the escapees or pretending that we didn't see their departure. A few nuggets of child-rearing wisdom are doled out on the spot by family members whose names I will not expose.

The third kid has hung around long enough to slouch so low in his chair that he has slid the tablecloth (and his plate) down with him. Our siblings' children stay seated and clean their plates, wordlessly highlighting their cousins' poor form. They receive what in the moment feels like unnecessary levels of praise for their hearty appetites. Our siblings offer helpful tips on how to improve table etiquette with charts and stickers. Great-aunts and -uncles begin regaling us with stories of how other people in the family had terrible table manners as children, too. "Like they'd been locked up in a cave or something. Ha, ha," they laugh. "Maybe it's genetic."

While clearing plates my husband looks for someone to blame. I had been on the verge of pinning it all on him, too, but he was just quicker. "Well, maybe if we didn't feed them for a few nights, they'd start to appreciate food and they'd be inclined to stay at the table." I am about to offer my own observations on the matter until I opt instead for a deep breath and a mantra or two. I look at the situation again. Nobody meant any harm; they just are very generous with their opinions. They adore the kids. Thanksgiving dinner around here usually lasts for only two hours.

No matter how much we love our families, raising children with them or under their direct gaze can be challenging. The mantras in the following section are designed to reframe situations with the main players (parents, siblings, and partners) so that we feel less distressed in those relationships and more competent in our roles as mothers. Mantras can't dissipate all of the conflicts that infiltrate even the best relationships, but they can (with the help of a large glass of wine) get you through a holiday meal unscathed.

Chapter 12

. . .

Our Parents
(but Mostly Our Mothers)

Here's how I imagined it would go. I would give birth to a child.
Upon laying eyes on this child, all of his grandparents would
have something akin to a religious experience. This would be the
event they had waited for their entire lives. Quite frankly, they
just wouldn't see the world the same way any longer. Of course,
after the encounter, they would be incapable of squandering one
moment of their lives away from this new person. Would they

want to miss the first smile, the first step, the first word? No way! Some of them, the heartier ones, those better suited to heftier child-care responsibilities, might even be moved to quit their jobs or at least drastically scale back. They would do all of these things at their own behest. I would do no more prompting than have the child and wait for their arrival. In my mind I would roll my eyes in a loving, bemused manner, letting my husband in on the joke, as the grandparents bickered over who would fill the tot's weekends with educational and recreational activities. After about a year, sentences like "We insist, you two *need* to get away for the weekend" would fill the air. I would mock-scold them, "If you don't let me see him sometimes, he'll forget that I'm his mother!" Laughter would ensue. We would all bask in our collective love for this child. There would never be the panicked feeling so common to the mother caught up in the babysitting juggling act, because one of them would always be available at a moment's notice.

No matter that these grandparents were scattered across the globe. That they were all gainfully employed—and relied on their incomes for survival. Never you mind that some had remarried and were raising new families. So what if my husband and I have siblings with children, and they too wouldn't mind a little help here and there. All of these impediments would be resolved upon the arrival of this baby.

In real life, they sent gifts. They were concerned about the baby's and mother's health. They were all thrilled to be grandparents. But their world did not assume a new orbit. Furthermore, the fantasy took a nasty knock regarding the maternal grandmother. I had entertained special hopes for this particular grandparent (my mother), since she is the youngest of the four and really likes taking care of children. True to form, my mom was and is great. If I'm in a pinch, she'll drive hours to lend a hand. But by the third day, she's got her luggage neatly piled by the door. She eats breakfast and soon thereafter she's just a cloud of dust in the road. In my fantasy I envisioned her in the kitchen (when it was convenient for me) making bread. Or at the kitchen table helping a child with a math sheet. My mom would give her life for her kids and grandchildren—like if they needed a kidney or lung. But let's face it: my mother is busy with a full-time job, a packed social life, and until recently the job of caring for her aging mother. The role of grandmother is an important one to her, but, unfortunately for my fantasy, not the only one in her life.

Aside from having our fantasies dashed upon the rocks of how much time our parents will devote to helping us raise our children, a whole new batch of issues often surfaces when we have children. Prior to my having children, my parents and I had reached a civil sort of "don't ask, don't tell" plateau in our relationship. I made my choices, they made theirs. We peacefully co-existed in parallel universes. But suddenly having a swarm of children spilling milk on your mother's floor, grinding crackers into her carpet, and dumping all of her collectible (or used to be) glass figurines into a laundry basket is bound to change the dynamics of the relationship. Perhaps your mother didn't have much advice regarding your career as a loan officer, but she most likely will have a few tips on how to raise her grandchildren. Even if she doesn't come right out and say it, you'll *know* what she's thinking.

The following mantras are designed to bring a sense of levity and balance to relationships that by their nature can trigger extreme emotional states. They are meant to help us find our footing within our new roles. (My very good friend and her husband actually evicted her mother two days after the birth of their son, all the while shouting, "Stop telling us what to do. We're the parents now!!!") These mantras can be used during phone calls, drop-by visits, or extended family vacations to dude ranches. However, a few additional safeguards should be in place prior to close contact between three or more generations for extended time periods. Meditate daily. Bolster each mantra with five or six deep breaths. Practice ongoing states of focused compassion and forgiveness toward your parents and yourself. And finally, take very long trips to the grocery store—alone.

· Take what they can give ·

Perhaps the best advice I ever got during my training regarding creating healthier relationships with one's own parents came from a gifted family therapist named Pat Colucci. Pat had trained under Betty Carter, a pioneer in family systems therapy and the director of The Family Institute of Westchester in New York. In our training, Pat taught us that a telltale sign therapy had really clicked occurred when a client was able to see a parent as a real person. In this process, unproductive fantasies and expectations were relinquished in favor of constructing a reality-based relationship, functional in spite of its limitations and flaws. Sounds simple, but think how many unresolved feelings we often carry around with us from our childhoods. Many of these dynamics continue to color our adult relationships with our parents. Old resentments and emotions linger on, often blocking us from relating nonreactively with our parents. As long as we ask our parents to be present for us in ways that exceed their abilities or comfort zones, we are setting ourselves up for even more disappointment.

According to Murray Bowen, a preeminent family systems theorist, one of the most toxic processes in any family is a cutoff, an extreme disengagement or distancing from the system until there is no involvement. In their work *The Changing Family Life*

Cycle, Betty Carter and Monica McGoldrick, followers of Bowen, write: "Cutoff robs families of their essence and vitality, and contributes a sense of hollowness and vulnerability to the individual members it launches." One of the techniques Pat used to prevent cutoffs involved coaching clients to ask their parent(s) for something they were capable of giving. From a systems perspective, this provides a restorative experience and, in short, organizes and repairs the system. Rather than emotionally cutting off from parents who are unable to "get it all right," we create healthier relationships by asking for *what they can give. Asking for what they can give* means that we don't compare our parents to some idealized version of who they are. We stop comparing notes about what our friends' mothers do. Creating a healthful and sustainable relationship with our parents, for everyone's sake, requires us to *ask for what they can give.*

Of course we are adults with our own children; we aren't utterly dependent on our parents any longer. But a healthy family system depends on intergenerational connection. We give, we receive. *Taking what they can give* allows our parents to be connected to our children in a healthy, role-appropriate manner. If your parents can't watch your children for the entire day, maybe an hour or two is what you can ask for. One of my friends, Julia, has a mother who is a busy executive. For a long time Julia resented that her mother never changed a diaper or wiped a snotty nose. When she heard the mantra *take what they can give*, she asked her mom if she'd like to come by with takeout dinners once a week. Now, Julia gets a break from cooking. Her mother feels like she's making a contribution, and the kids see a functional model for how three generations care for one another. *Take what they can give* broadens the channel between our parents, ourselves, and our children. Rather than being held hostage to unrealistic demands or expectations, we become open to meeting our parents where they are and accepting the gifts they can offer.

· I survived ·

Sometimes help from our parents comes in mysterious ways and with heart-stopping twists we may be better off not knowing about. But when we ask our parents to *grab an end* (a mantra coming later in the book), within reason, we also have to practice letting go. Until very recently, all four of my husband's and my parents were suspicious of the need for car seats. The logic of a playpen they got (in fact, we recently learned that both sets of parents actually drove around with us inside playpens, slamming against the rails as they barreled through corners). But car seats? "Who needs 'em?" they'd mutter defensively after getting caught driving the kids around like a bunch of free-range chickens. "When you were young, we'd just throw you in the backseat and off we went. It takes four hours to buckle everyone in for a three-minute drive to the grocery store. You never rode in a car seat and you survived." True. But put them in the damn car seat next time.

Jenny had recently moved to a small New England town much closer to where her aging, though very spry, parents lived. Much to her surprise, they came up for a week and offered to take care of the kids while Jenny unpacked and moved things into their new house. Just as they promised, her parents came by at eight in the morning, loaded the children up, and headed off for a nearby beach. Jenny thought to shout admonitions about sunscreen but checked herself. At one her parents returned for lunch without the children. Jenny met them at the door with a stunned face. "*WHERE ARE THE KIDS?*" Her mother patted her hand and walked in the door. "Well, dear, we had breakfast at the cutest restaurant and met the loveliest waitress who *also happens* to babysit. I told her that you were looking for help. Luckily, she was just finishing her shift and so she took them to the park for a few hours. We're due to pick them up soon, so we should have lunch rather quickly." About fifty-two different responses came careening through Jenny's head. Instead of falling to the floor crying and asking her mother why she had handed her children off to a total stranger, she took a deep breath and reminded herself that this was the woman responsible for raising her, she trusted her judgment implicitly, and *she had survived.*

I survived doesn't mean we give our kids over to parents who aren't stable or responsible enough to care for them. Another friend won't let her father stay alone with her children because his anger is often expressed explosively, creating a physically and emotionally unsafe environment for her kids. But *I survived* is a reminder to trust our parents' guts, too. It's a call to allow them, so long as everyone is buckled up, the opportunity to participate in raising these children in their own way. I'll never forget entering the room and looking over at my four-month-old son (who had never ingested anything but breast milk) as my well-intentioned father shoveled an ice cream sundae into his mouth. Before one word could come out of my mouth, I stepped back, watched the baby's jaw drop open as a cue for more ice cream to be put in, and reminded myself that just like me, *he'll survive*. We were all happier for it.

In case you're wondering, the babysitter turned out to be, just as her mother stated, a lovely woman who continues to take care of Jenny's children to this day.

· Dodge the bullet ·

Note: Before reading this mantra, it would be helpful to picture in your mind the movie *The Matrix*. You'll get the point without having seen it. But it would be like playing a video game with no visuals—the effect will be noticeably diminished.

Claudia's mother emigrated from Germany in the 1950s and raised her children very strictly, without a lot of effusive emotional displays of affection—like hugging. At the age of eighty, she still hasn't warmed up that much. Claudia is a devoted daughter, although there is a price to pay for her fealty. Once a month, she loads her two children and her husband into the car and drives four hours to visit. They stay at a hotel and eat all of their meals out so as not to disturb her mother's routine. Her children are the most well behaved kids on the planet. Bar none. They stay for only two days at a stretch, and the whole time the family walks on eggshells. Last month, Claudia was sucking down the dregs of milk in her children's cups when her mom left the room so they wouldn't get yelled at for wasting food. Yet without fail, Claudia's mother gets in at least two good zingers before the trip is over. Recently, the slights have been directed at Claudia's six-year-old son, whose anxiety is triggered by close contact with his grandmother. He becomes stiff and reluctant to speak for fear of saying the wrong thing. This inspired Claudia's mother to ask in German, "Claudia, what's wrong with the boy? Is he dumb?" (I understand from Claudia that in German this word has a very nasty feeling to it.)

Claudia used to spend the entire trip tense and on edge about when the zingers would come. Normally quite composed, Claudia found herself reactive and resentful about her mother's attempts to hit the jugular. She seemed to enjoy the rise she could predictably get out of Claudia. Now, however, Claudia *dodges the bullet*. She sees her mother line up for the shot and instantly puts everything in slow motion. The bullet leaves her mother's mouth and heads right for her. Rather than being shot in the heart, she takes on the smooth, balletic moves of the *Matrix* guy. She leans backward in a gravity-defying position and *dodges the bullet*, which zips by her shoulder and punctures a nearby tree.

Of course Claudia could imagine herself as Buddha practicing compassion toward her mother. She could choose to see her mother's fear and anger as a call for love, respect, and acceptance. She could see these arrows as the responses of a woman so paralyzed that she can function only within a small, usually negative, range of emotions. And she still can. *Dodging the bullet* doesn't mean that we don't frame these interactions in a larger context. Understanding why our parents do some of the things they do helps firm our commitment to nonreaction. But visualizing yourself clad in black leather, slickly outmaneuvering any dangerous barbs headed your way, can evoke a feeling of control, particularly when someone is playing on our fears and insecurities.

Dodging the bullet is what we do when we're under fire. It reduces our urge to fire back. *Dodge the bullet* doesn't mean that we don't set boundaries with our parents, letting them fire away at will. Claudia eventually told her mother that she needed to be more careful about what she said in front of the kids, since their

German was improving. Plus, it just wasn't a nice way to treat your grandchildren. But the mantra does help us take control of how we respond to difficult situations with our parents (or anyone, for that matter). As the Dalai Lama writes, "Deep within the human being abides the wisdom that can support him or her in the face of negative situations. In this way, events no longer throw him because he is holding the reins."

· WW__D ·

When I ran a mental health clinic in East Harlem, one of the social workers, Pauline, wore a bracelet on which was inscribed the letters WWJD. I asked Pauline what it meant, and she told me it stood for "What Would Jesus Do?" Genius, I thought. Here was a constant reminder to practice love, forgiveness, generosity, and peace. I wanted to get one for every kid in the clinic. As a fist was raised for the first blow of the fight, the child would catch sight of the bracelet, reframe the situation within the qualities mentioned above, and recall his conflict resolution skills. Skirmish averted. However, the principal informed me that the separation of church and state issue might be tricky.

I think this mantra, or some variation of it, offers a powerful and grounding sentiment for all of us in the crossroads of a mothering decision. Sometimes it helps to look outside of ourselves and align our intentions with someone who stands for the qualities we are trying to embrace. However, it may be particularly valuable for those of us who grew up without consistent or nurturing mother figures in our lives. This absence may have occurred through death or due to a mother's psychological unavailability. Raised without a mother, we may be less likely to *trust our gut* because we feel that some valuable piece of information was not transmitted to us. In her book *Motherless Daughters*, Hope Edelman discusses the fears that many motherless women have that they simply won't know how to care for their children once they arrive. One woman in her study writes, "There are so many things about being a woman, a daughter, and a mother that I don't know and can't see any way for me to learn." Although motherless daughters have suffered a genuine and deep loss, the truth is that many of us question our ability to "get mothering right." This is true even if we had the most loving and supportive mother in the world.

Fortunately, mindful mothering isn't passively bestowed through the gene pool like height or hair color. Nor is it necessarily the product of watching how others mother, although this can be instructive. Mindful mothering is the intentional cultivating of love, patience, and kindness. When we need to be inspired or guided toward these characteristics, there are plenty of role models there for the taking. The mother of a friend died when she was eight, but she was blessed by a loving and highly involved grandmother. Now when she needs a touchstone for a mothering choice, she asks, *"What would Nana Jane do?"* I have used this mantra many times. After a child has begun pouring milk while watching television and not the cup, I pause and ask, *What would Buddha do?* Would Buddha go crazy over milk on the floor even if this is the third time this week? I doubt it. And when I need to practice compassion I ask, *What would Mother Teresa do?* For different situations I call forth different people, such as my very loving aunts, or my fearless sister, or my patient mother, or my wise father, or my humorous friends, or my irreverent husband. It can be Jesus or anyone else who in the moment of choice can point the way to the qualities conducive to mindful mothering.

Chapter 13

• • •

Sibling Rivalry
(and Not Between Your Kids)

The sibling relationship is likely to be the longest across the life-span. We can spend upward of seventy years knowing our brothers and sisters. For some of us, this might seem like a very long time indeed. Even though we're adults, the sibling rivalry of our youth often doesn't evaporate once we have children; it simply changes shape. Stephen Bond and Michael Kahn, authors of *Sibling Bond*, point out that throughout adolescence and into adulthood siblings struggle for superiority regarding issues of achievement/success, sexuality/beauty, and social relations within and outside of the family. As with any family dynamic, the power of our sibling relationships is not confined simply to the main players once we have children. One woman I know felt so belittled and tormented during her childhood by her older brothers that she refused to let her sons have any contact with them. Her older brothers, who had mellowed out considerably, used this to ratify their beliefs that their sister was "high-strung and difficult." The cutoff left her children confused and upset over not being able to visit their cousins.

The following mantras are designed to help cultivate some peace within the sibling bond based on our new roles. They may not undo years of being locked in a closet or being told that your sister was the "pretty one" and you "had kind eyes," but they may offer more effective ways to cope than pulling off the arms of all her Barbies.

· Take two! ·

I'd like to say that I grew up in a home with no sibling rivalry, but my sister is still alive and can vividly recall the times I chased her down the street with scissors and buried all of her shoes in the backyard. In retaliation for the latter offense, she plucked every last leaf off my mother's fifteen-year-old jade plant and hid them under my bed so that my mother would accidentally stumble across the "evidence" and blame me. This was not a relationship where feelings were spared out of some largesse or nod to the sibling bond. We looked at my mother like she was on drugs when she pleaded, "Sisters don't punch each other." Throughout adolescence, flaws were mentally noted, filed, artfully synthesized, and then launched during the next big fight. I was the classic first-born overachiever and she was the warmhearted, social second child. To this day, people in our family are stunned at how different we are, yet since having children we've never been closer. And it has everything to do with being mothers.

My sister and I had our first children less than a month apart, so there was plenty of fodder for ongoing competition and comparison. The ground was particularly ripe for it, given our circumstances. My sister was unmarried, still in graduate school, and had no health insurance. I had been married for five years, hustled my husband through law school, and begged him to get gainfully employed so we could have a baby. After my initial hysteria at finding out she was pregnant before me (*Me!*, who deserved to be pregnant much more due to the careful planning and foresight of an eldest child), something shifted. On a very profound level, we understood even without discussing it that if we wanted to create a healthier relationship, a radical shift had to occur in the way we dealt with each other. For the first time, there was something real at stake to deter our competition—our children. To some extent, the sudden change was fairly easy because we had a neutral new topic: pregnancy, something we were equally clueless about. Looking back, it was as though a director had walked in, clapped the do-hickey you see in movies about movies, and shouted, "*Take two*."

Take two is a reminder that no matter how fraught with conflict our relationships with our siblings have been, becoming mothers (or fathers) offers an opportunity to connect to them in a new way on unmarked territory. Maybe earlier in your lives you had the script to make a good relationship, the director (your mother) was giving you plenty of input, and maybe even the stage was set properly. But the execution was off—filled with whatever undermines sibling relationships: jealousy, a sense of limited resources, or competition. *Take two* is a chance to do the scene right.

It makes sense that we would use the platform of mothering as the launching place for a new bond with our siblings, because to some extent we *are* new people. Nothing changes us more than mothering, often giving us greater perspective, compassion, capacity for forgiveness, and insight into who we are and where we come from. When comparisons surface between our children, either from our parents or myself, *take two* allows me to step back and see what's really going on. Every time I find myself slipping back into that rivalrous role with my sister, I use the mantra *take two* and come back to the new reality we've created as sisters.

· Let 'em loose ·

Sometimes negative interactional patterns are so deeply entrenched that the sibling relationship is unlikely to change dramatically without concerted effort from both sides. Strong forces in the family system, like the expectations and actions of our parents and grandparents, are often silently working to perpetuate contentious relationships between sibs. In the seventies, therapist and writer Selma Fraiberg and colleagues wrote a pivotal paper entitled "Ghosts in the Nursery: A Psychoanalytic Approach to the Problems of Impaired Infant-Mother Relationships." In it she writes, "The intruders from the past have taken up residence in the nursery, claiming tradition and right of ownership. They have been present at the christening for two or more generations. While no one has issued an invitation, the ghosts take up residence and conduct the rehearsal of the family tragedy from a tattered script." These ghosts come in many forms and allude to patterns of abuse or neglect, alcoholism, mental illness, or any other force that threatens to erode the health and strength of the family. Although Fraiberg is specifically addressing the mother-child bond in her article, there is no question that these destructive intergenerational patterns infiltrate the entire family system. And the sibling bond is no exception.

Melanie was one of four children. From earliest memory, she and her siblings had been locked in an ongoing battle to win their emotionally distant parents' approval. The siblings perpetually belittled one another and craftily sabotaged each other's feelings of self-worth. Things didn't improve measurably once they moved out and started their own families. When Melanie gave birth to her eldest daughter, her sister called to wish her congratulations. When she heard that Melanie had named her daughter Jade, she laughed and cuttingly asked, "What if the next one is a boy? How about Quartz or Limestone?" At that point, the light went on. Melanie was able to see the ghosts that undermined her sister's and brothers' ability to be loving and supportive without traces of derision and scorn. She could see clearly the toxic and competitive environment in which her parents raised them. Melanie came to the conclusion that to keep her connection with her siblings, she had to *let 'em loose*. This may sound contradictory, but it's not. It was as though she had three wild horses on tethers. The closer she tried to pull them in to "fix" the relationships, the more she got trampled. *By letting them loose*, she was not casting them from her life; she was simply shifting her proximity to their thrashing hooves.

When Melanie decided to *let 'em loose*, she found that she was free to focus her energy and attention on building relationships with her nieces and nephews. In doing so, Melanie avoided cutting off and emotionally disengaging from the sibling system—an unhealthy choice bound to perpetuate the creation of more ghosts for her own children. *Let 'em loose* allows us to gently and mindfully place the sibling connection on the back burner while we tend to our relationships with their children. In a way, it's a chance to let go of the ghosts and focus on the healthy relationships we can cultivate with our siblings' children.

It is important to note that this mantra isn't a call to cut off, ignore, or intentionally distance ourselves from our siblings. Nor is it justifying acting passive-aggressively toward our siblings by flaunting a preference for their children. That isn't the spirit of the mantra. Instead, *let 'em loose* asks us to recognize that we may never create the happy, loving, loyal sibling bond we've heard is possible, but that isn't a deal breaker. *Let 'em loose* allows us to shift our emotional proximity–seeking toward our siblings' offspring (or our siblings' relationship to our children). A psychologist friend of mind recalled how her mother and aunt were on the verge of completely disengaging from each other. Their relationship was salvaged only after she was born and her aunt developed a close relationship with her. By *letting 'em loose*, we're still committed to honoring the power of the family system; we're just giving our siblings a little more rope to keep from getting tangled up.

Chapter 14

. . .

Our Partners

Marriage was easy before we had kids. My husband and I lived abroad and traveled. We ate out in restaurants and went to movies. We spoke to each other in complete sentences about the intricacies of our careers and world affairs. In the evenings we would go for long runs in Riverside Park. This went on for five blissful years. I can't say that our marriage has taken any serious hits by having the children. In fact, as with any brothers-in-arms, our service has probably deepened our bond. But there have been marked changes in our union. We never sleep alone or naked, yet there are plenty of half-clothed bodies in our bed each night. We rarely eat out, although it is my husband's true joy. (This is a man who took a week off from work and attended the Culinary Institute of America. In our early twenties, he made me, a heavily pregnant woman, forgo three meals in a row while traveling in France to save enough money for a dinner at a three-star restaurant.) This fine man has been reduced to eating the ends of hot dogs (shunned by our kids) and leftover pasta from the pot on the stove for dinner. The last time we exercised together was when we were in graduate school. But we find ways to survive life in the foxhole, such as talking on the phone like adolescent girls when we should be working.

No doubt about it, marriage or any partnership gets tougher after the babies descend. There's just a lot more work, a lot more stress, and a lot less time for each other (and a lot more joy, but we don't really need mantras for that). The mantras in this section are designed to help us cope more effectively with the demands mothering places on our marriages and partnerships. In doing so, we connect more powerfully to what is undoubtedly our best support system.

· Ignore the score ·

As a young graduate student and newlywed I remember scorning the studies we were reading in our family therapy class about how the lion's share of household chores falls on the woman and the stress this caused. "Not so in our house," I would mutter smugly, watching my husband haul the laundry out of our fourth-floor walk-up and down seven blocks to the laundromat. "Don't forget to use bleach this time, either! Let's see if we can get those whites to sparkle!" I would yell behind him. Oh yes, things were pretty even in our home regarding cooking and cleaning. One day, after I had finished bragging about our household equities, my very smart mentor and dissertation adviser looked at me with a bemused smile and said as though auguring the future, "Just wait until you have children."

I must admit, I see what she means. When my husband is pressured at work, he catches an early train to the office to get a handle on things. When my schedule heats up, I have the added pleasure of begging someone to pick up my kids from school and baseball, scraping together makeshift babysitting arrangements, and cooking in advance for the meals I'll miss. Sure, my husband pitches in, but there are a thousand little household chores that he doesn't even know exist. (You pack them lunch? Every day?)

Because he's the primary breadwinner, there is always the underlying belief that his job is more essential to the survival of the family. There may be some truth to this, but it often doesn't seem fair. You may have picked up on the fact that a lot of things about mothering aren't fair, rational, or avoidable. However, dwelling on the unfairness of the situation does little to exorcise my anger or change my circumstances.

John Gottman is the nation's leading marital researcher. In his book *Why Marriages Succeed or Fail*, Gottman details the communication styles that undermine a healthy marriage. He calls these toxic interactions "The Four Horsemen of the Apocalypse," and they are *criticism, contempt, defensiveness*, and *stonewalling*. Although within all marriages these behaviors surface from time to time, marriages high in these four patterns of communication tend to fail. More specifically, if the ratio of positive to negative communications between spouses is five to one or better, the marriage is likely to succeed. Less than that and you've got trouble. In one study, Gottman and his colleagues were able to predict with an impressive 94 percent accuracy from a marital history and the couple's current view of their marriage whether the marriage would be intact in three years.

Not surprisingly, Gottman cites sex and housework as the two biggest marital hot spots. (Unfortunately, sex exceeds the scope of this book. But if it helps, my French friend uses the mantra *why not?*) So how do resentment and anger over housework lead to strained marriages? Gottman writes: "The more wives complain and criticize, the more husbands withdraw and stonewall; the more husbands withdraw and stonewall, the more wives complain and criticize. This cycle must be broken if conflict-engaging marriages are to avoid dissolution." To remedy this loop of tension, Gottman has great advice. He encourages men to assume more responsibilities and women to gently confront their husbands about what needs doing around the house. He also cautions women to avoid *kitchen-sinking*—a contemptuous summary of all of her past and present complaints. Gottman also urges both partners to use self-soothing, non–distress maintaining thoughts about the conflict—something a lot like a mantra. These "reframes" help us gain greater perspective over a situation and reduce the likelihood of getting swept away by the four horsemen.

The multitasking madness of motherhood often leaves us reeling with the sheer amount of work we have to do. Sometimes I go to bed feeling like I only got a small fraction of it done. When I'm particularly overwhelmed, I get resentful and critical (a horseman) of my husband. A dangerous internal dialogue begins taking shape. "Why do I have to do *everything* around here? Why can't he help more—at least not leave his dishes in the sink for me to wash like I'm the den mother." This, I believe, is what Gottman refers to as kitchen-sinking. The longer this negative script develops, the more defensive (another horseman) I become and in danger of assuming what Gottman calls the "innocent-victim" role—meaning "I am faultless in all of this and you are a total thoughtless jerk." Each time I find myself headed down this slippery slope, I do two things—both recommended by Gottman. First, I gently ask him to do a specific list of things with no derision—well, sometimes there is scorn, but he's a big man and he usually lets it slide.

Second, I practice the mantra *ignore the score*. *Ignore the score* is a reminder that keeping track of "he did, she did" leads me nowhere but down the road of frustration and resentment. It's okay to ask for help, but the reality is that mothering will never be a totally fair and equitable endeavor. Sometimes even asking for help can't change it. Furthermore, the harder and longer I look at the scorecard, the more myopic my vision gets. I stop noticing what my husband *is* doing to help. A recent study in the *Journal of Family Therapy* notes that men actually do more housework (men's actual contribution: 39 percent) than we give them credit for (our estimation: 33 percent), although they give themselves more credit than they deserve (their estimation: 42 percent). *Ignore the score* is a reminder to step out of the innocent-victim role that undermines our happiness and well-being. When it comes to rectifying the unfairness of mothering, ask for help, *ignore the score*, and leave the laundry in a place where it's hard for your partner to overlook.

· Let go of the tick ·

Annabelle reluctantly went on vacation with her husband and their daughter to the Berkshires in western Massachusetts. She went with some reservation because her idea of a vacation involved room service, a minifridge in the room, and a nearby spa. What she got instead was a tent and an outdoor latrine. Annabelle and her husband agreed on the destination because they both believed that if they were going to raise their young daughter in the city, they should at least ensure that she had some exposure, however brief and sporadic, to nature. Annabelle felt a great sense of relief as they piled their camping equipment back into the car and headed home.

The next morning Annabelle's four-year-old daughter, Celia, woke screaming at the top of her lungs. When Annabelle and her husband ran into the room to see what had happened, they found Celia clawing at her neck, screaming, "Something is on me! It won't come off." When they pulled up her long black hair they found a tick the size of a rain-soaked raisin. Annabelle's husband, James, is from a ranch in Montana, where he was regularly infested with ticks in his youth. According to James, the way to extricate a tick is to take a searing pin and touch the body of the tick. Upon feeling the scorch of the pin, the tick will unburrow from its host's body. To say that Annabelle was highly suspicious of the proposed technique is to put it mildly. She advocated pulling the thing out with tweezers. But James was adamant. "You want the thing out or not?" he demanded as though there were only two choices—fire pin or permanent infestation. "Well, yes," Annabelle replied with some concern. "All right then, I'll go heat the needle." And he flew out of the room.

Annabelle took this as her cue to release her hysterical child and run for the tweezers. She was hoping to have the tick out by the time he returned, rendering his witch doctoring unnecessary. Annabelle returned and placed Celia on her lap. Although she got hold of the tick, it was in too deep for her to remove it. When James ran back into the room with his glowing needle, Annabelle at first refused to surrender their daughter. "Hurry," he demanded. "I gotta get this on him before it cools off." Celia, seeing a hot needle coming at her neck, screamed louder and tried to jerk out of Annabelle's grasp. "What next?" Annabelle thought. "Leeches for fevers? Perhaps coining or cupping for infection?" With great skepticism and grave concern for her daughter, Annabelle *let go of the tick* and held her daughter down for her husband. Holding a thrashing toddler still enough for a man with moderate fine-motor skills to apply the tip of a pin to a tick is not easy. Sure enough, the pin got lodged in Celia's neck, which ratcheted up her hysteria. Now she was tick-infested, pricked, and most likely burned.

Several times Annabelle wanted to scream, "Enough, you crackpot!" But a big source of tension in their marriage centered around James's complaint that Annabelle undermined him in front of the children. Plus, Annabelle quite sensibly concluded that watching her parents argue would only serve to agitate Celia even more. So Annabelle resisted her urge to scream, told herself to *let go of the tick*, and held on firmly to her daughter. In the bigger picture, she also reminded herself that Celia most likely *would survive*. After about three more attempts, James confirmed that the tick was in too deep for even a method as effective as the flaming pin. They decided to take Celia to the pediatrician, where it took three nurses holding her down and a specialized pair of tweezers to rid her of the intruder. Annabelle felt vindicated when the doctor looked at her in disbelief when she inquired if he had ever run across her husband's hot-pin method in medical school.

When parenting, it often happens that my husband and I have equally strong but opposing views on how to tackle a situation. For the sake of our marriage and for our children, I am required to practice letting go. Letting go means putting aside my need to be right, to control the situation, to be the final authority, to have all the right answers. Jon Kabat-Zinn states that "letting go means to give up coercing, resisting, or struggling, in exchange for something more powerful and wholesome." Sometimes, re-specting our partner's role and participation in our child's life means *letting go of the tick.* In doing so, we validate and accept our partner as essential and worthwhile. Giving our partners the authority to parent equally keeps us from marginalizing their involvement—a complaint that many non–primary caregivers express. I'm not always good at this. Most of the time I am responsible for making the choices about the kids—what they eat, discipline, deciding how loud is too loud. But *let go of the tick* is a reminder that I need to pass the power over sometimes, even in the moments when it's hardest to do.

Put it in park

Note: While anyone can use this mantra, it is particularly practical for use with spouses who are no longer our spouses.

Things for Emma and her ex-husband, Gary, had been going from bad to worse. It hadn't been a great marriage in the first place, so it wasn't surprising that the aftermath wasn't particularly peaceable either. Shortly after the divorce, Gary seemed to forget that he'd actually fathered a child. Like clockwork, Emma would get a call Friday nights from Gary saying he had to work late and wouldn't be able to make it. This would devastate their son, Adam, and infuriate Emma. She tried not to show her disgust and resentment in front of her son, but such intense feelings were often difficult to conceal.

Visits between Gary and Adam had become virtually nonexistent. Adam still talked to his dad on the phone every week and begged to see him. Secretly, Emma was glad not to have to deal with Gary's lame excuses and be forced to put her son back together after another disappointing no-show. Plus, she was enjoying a little vacation from the dark moods that descended whenever she interacted with her ex-husband. So she was neither pleased to hear from him nor eager to resume visitations when Gary resurfaced after a six-month hiatus. Gary called on a Wednesday evening and Adam answered the phone. When he told his son about the great weekend he had planned for them, Adam instantly began pleading with his mother to let him go. After threatening Gary with serious physical harm if he screwed this up, Emma consented. "Just tell me your new address and I'll drop him off Friday," Emma said stiffly. There was a pause. Emma waited while she heard Gary cover the receiver and whisper to someone in the room.

Finally, Gary broke the silence by suggesting to Emma that they meet in a supermarket parking lot, as it would be more convenient for him. "More convenient than if I drop him off at your door? What are you talking about? Look, I'm not sure what you're up to and I don't really care. But I'm not dropping my son off in a parking lot like some kidnapper. Forget it." As her volume began to rise, she saw her son looking at her with tears rolling down his face. Emma took a deep breath, assessed the situation, and said, "Fine. What time?" Emma really *had* stopped being invested in what Gary did with his personal life, but she did mind that his inability to be a responsible parent continued to take such an emotional toll on their son and her.

When Emma pulled into the parking lot, she saw Gary getting out of a new sports car. Inside was the woman Emma accused him of having an affair with during their marriage, despite his sworn protests to the contrary. In Gary's bizarre logic, he must have thought that if Emma didn't see where they lived, she wouldn't figure out they were living together. The fact that he put her through this charade to conceal that he was shacking up with someone was like gasoline on fire. The moment Emma saw Gary, she felt an incredible urge to run over him—even just a little—perhaps brushing his hip or accidentally rolling over his foot. The urge was so strong that she decided it would be safer to park the car and walk over to where he was waiting. In fact, the impulse to flatten him was so enticing, she had to repeat the mantra *put it in park* over and over before she could let go of the idea.

Emma survived the encounter (as did Gary) but held on to the mantra *put it in park*. Although the desire to crush him with her Honda never resurfaced to the extent it did in the parking lot that day, she found that the mantra helped her manage the extreme anger that often surfaced in connection with him. Quite simply, Emma was tired of losing control and knew that her animosity toward Gary wasn't healthy for Adam. Supporting Emma's gut feeling is John Gottman's finding that marital conflict, particularly a wife's scorn and contempt for her husband, has a powerfully negative effect on children. Interestingly, one of the buffers they identified in protecting kids against the fallout of a conflicted marriage is the "inhibition of negative parental affect." Basically, this means the more we can stem our feelings of bitterness and anger, the better off our kids will be.

Now when Emma wants to choke Gary for being three hours late to pick up Adam (he finally let go of the secret drop-off spots once he got busted), she whispers the mantra *put it in park* and sends Adam happily down the walkway. When she wants to eviscerate him for being two months late with child support while buying his girlfriend a new home gym, she reminds herself to *put it in park. Put it in park* doesn't mean we don't act assertively and speak up for the best interests of our child. It does mean that we check our impulses to rant and rave at our ex-spouses or spouses (even if justified) in front of our kids, because we know the price. *Put it in park* is a call to avoid delving over and over again into a source of anger that gets us nowhere and solves none of our problems. Plus *put it in park* has the added benefit of keeping us out of jail.

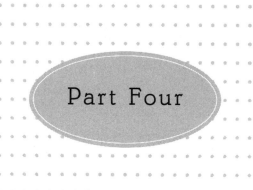

Part Four

Who
We
Are

In a storefront window on West End Avenue I catch a glimpse of myself. It is an oppressive 98-degree day in New York City. I am pushing a double stroller with three wet towels draped around my shoulders after an afternoon of sprinklers that have been sadistically embedded in searing pavement. There is a smear of chocolate ice cream on my neck. Hair is plastered to the side of my face. Sweat drips into my eyes, burning them with the sunscreen I have slathered on myself and my youth. Muscles in my eyes bulge as I struggle to push three kids up the 79th Street hill in a stroller with the aerodynamics of a cement truck. As I look at my reflection, I am shocked and frightened. Only five years ago, men looked at me with some degree of interest. Now I detect a heavy dose of pity. Perhaps some are looking inward and asking themselves, "Should I help this lady who is loaded down like a mule with her stroller?" However, I am quite sure from their expressions that nobody is thinking *anything* lascivious.

It happens fast. For most of us, the role of mother moves to the fore of our identity almost as soon as we get our hands on the baby. Pre-kids we identify ourselves in a multitude of ways: by our professions, our personality characteristics, race, ethnicity, religion, appearance, loyalties, interests, social or political beliefs, qualities we are endowed with, and places we hail from. Post-kids those qualities still exist. But by and large, mothering seems to eclipse everything we once thought was most salient about who we are. At the very least, mothering changes the way we operate in the world.

Mothering even creeps into the child-free areas of our lives. A friend of mine noticed that at our Sunday night ice-hockey games if we smash into another player we immediately try to hoist her up as though she were a newborn antelope, all the while saying, "Oh my God, I'm so sorry. Are you okay?" Trust me: we never did this in college. Our elevated empathy levels now require us to think about injuries, impairments, and trips to the ER. My friend describes this phenomenon as having been mutated by motherhood. We are no longer just hockey players; we are hockey-playing *mothers*.

· I took the vow ·

Jessica was an actress before she had children. We're not talking an extra on daytime television commercials, either. She was a trained, accomplished, serious actress. She and her husband, William, would sit on the couch at night and perform the role of the building superintendent in fifteen dialects. They can tell you which languages are glottal in nature. After she had her first child, Jessica gave up her theater career and became a full-time stay-at-home mother. There are very few professions in which people stand up and clap for you every night, throw flowers, and ask for your autograph when you have finished your shift. Mothering is not one of them.

The other day I was in Jessica's house and I looked at my friend digging ruefully into a massive pile of laundry strewn on the kitchen table. Dirty dishes were waiting to be washed. Kids were pulling on her pant legs telling her that the cat had puked on one of their beds. It would have looked just like my house, except behind her on the wall was a giant photograph of her dolled up in glamorous clothes with perfectly coiffed hair, staring dramatically into her costar's eyes. Currently, she looked as if she had been delivered to the kitchen via hurricane. And I knew that when she finished cleaning, cooking, bathing, and folding, no one would be clapping and crying out her name for anything other than juice or for her to change the channel. We had been talking about the demands of mothering and she asked, "So, is this what it's all about? Is this who I am now?" "Yep," I replied. "Maybe you should take the pictures down so the difference is not so striking."

Like Jessica, we are all transformed to some extent by the reality of mothering. The experience of mothering is so consuming, it escapes virtually all comparisons. I had never come across any other endeavor that matched it until I read about the process of becoming a bodhisattva. In Tibetan Buddhism, a bodhisattva is an enlightened being who works to lead all humanity out of suffering and toward enlightenment. Buddhist teacher Chogyam Trungpa Rinpoche's description of taking the bodhisattva vow sounds uncannily like becoming a mother: "The bodhisattva vow is the commitment to put others before oneself. It is a statement to give up one's own well-being . . . for the sake of others. And a bodhisattva is simply a person who lives in the spirit of that vow, perfecting the qualities known as the six paramitas— generosity, discipline, patience, exertion, meditation, and transcendental knowledge." Later on he writes, "We [bodhisattvas] could be beaten, kicked, or just unappreciated, but we remain willing to work with others. It is a totally noncredit situation. It is truly very genuine and very powerful." Another feature of the bodhisattva vow is that once you take it, there's no backing out. Ring any bells?

The part about being beaten and kicked resonated strongly the other day as my two-year-old began expressing his displeasure with my limit-setting by beating me about the head and neck with his tiny fists. All the while, I held him at arm's length while his appendages rotated like the blades of a boat propeller and repeated the mantra *patience is my profession*. At the back of my mind, however, there was a more firmly entrenched mantra that is always whirring, *I took the vow*. *I took the vow* is a reminder that motherhood is often unpleasant and demanding, but that's okay. I *chose* it; it didn't *happen* to me. I accepted it into my life. I welcomed it (and most of the time I still do). Even if you didn't go into mothering willingly, you are here now. *I took the vow* galvanizes my mission. It reminds me that mothering isn't really supposed to be a vacation. This mantra reframes mothering for what it is—a life-altering challenge. No cakewalk, but the most worthwhile thing I've ever taken on.

We might read Trungpa's statement and take offense, as if sacrificing our own "well-being" goes against the admonition "you can't take care of others unless you are taking care of yourself." This is true, of course—in a very literal sense. And that issue will come up in a following section. The better off you are (healthier, rested, happier), the more you can nurture your children. But the larger spirit of the bodhisattva vow is similar to the vow of mothering—by choosing to become mothers, we set the stage to serve selflessly and unconditionally. We just do. *We took the vow.* No matter how we got to mothering, willingly or sideswiped by the whole affair, we are here.

The mother who falls down the stairs with her child takes the brunt of the collision by reflex. When resources are tight, we sacrifice so that our children's needs are met first. We think the flight attendant is nuts when she instructs us to put on our own oxygen mask before our child's. Typically, we sacrifice without question and with a brave spirit because the job can't really be done meaningfully any other way. By *taking the vow*, we are transformed into the bodhisattvas of motherhood. Mothering is truly an exercise in selflessness. But the mantras are a self-serving means to fulfill that role. *Just because we give ourselves over to mothering doesn't mean we have to lose ourselves in it.* So, dive into the sea of motherhood and let the mantras help keep your head above water.

Chapter 15

The Core Self

Mindful mothering requires us to *take the vow.* It asks us to serve fully. But that does not mean that we wipe out our larger being. While mothering may be a largely defining part of who we are, it is by no means *all* of who we are. Beyond our roles as mothers, wives, partners (or all of our relationships for that matter), our various identities, our feelings, and our thoughts, we find our fundamental nature. There are many ways to refer to this essential nature. Here, we'll call it the core Self. The capital S is used to denote its supremacy over all smaller components of our identity. The core Self is our most basic and essential being. According to Buddhist teachings, we are born into the world with all of the wisdom and goodness that we will ever have. We come fully equipped—*loaded*, if you will. As meditation instructor and writer Stephen Levine asserts, "There's nothing that is absent from our being which a Buddha or a Christ or a Mohammed possesses; it is the same well-spring, the same original nature, a shared essence." Rather than achieving or acquiring these qualities as we go through life, we find our own Buddha nature by connecting back to the core Self.

The core Self has two defining aspects. First, it is defined by the qualities of gentleness, compassion, love, strength, wisdom, goodness, and innocence. Second, these positive qualities of the core Self are constant and immutable. Without exception, the goodness and perfection of the core Self can't be polluted or destroyed. The core Self is defined by these elements throughout our lives regardless of the mistakes we make, no matter how many times we scream at our kids or do other things we later wish we hadn't. Beneath these harsh or unkind actions is a core of gentleness that is the foundation of who we *really* are. Unlike feelings, roles, or other identities that are always subject to change, the core Self is always present.

· No matter what ·

When teaching the notion of the core Self to at-risk and incarcerated youth, we get the usual what-ifs. "What if you robbed someone? What if you killed someone? What if you set something on fire and that set something *else* really big on fire? What if you stole your mother's rent money three months in a row? Is your core Self still good?" And the answer we offer is always the same: "*No matter what*, the power and goodness of the core Self is always there." We go on to explain that sometimes we can get pulled away from the core Self, thereby weakening its powers to guide and inform our choices and act in respectful, loving ways. We explain how it's essential to take responsibility for one's behavior. We stress making amends when possible. But we are clear: the power of the core Self can't be extinguished.

As you might imagine, being in prison can call into question one's self-worth. Sitting in a cell, one wonders, "Who am I *really*?" In my experience, mothering has the same effect. And mothering, perhaps more than any other venture, can generate feelings that really shake us up. We question our sanity as well as our identity. Screaming at our kids in the grocery store that if they pull one more thing off the shelf we will tie their hands to the cart may seem at odds with the notion of a good, wise, essential nature. In a moment of sleep-deprived delirium, my dear friend bit her two-year-old, who had just bitten her. These are extreme, dark feelings and actions. Even if we have managed not to act on these feelings, most of us have had them. But knowing, *no matter what*, the core of who we are remains good and loving, can strengthen us when we most need it. Understanding that our deepest nature is fundamentally gentle and kind—despite being driven to the edge—encourages us to pick ourselves up, make amends, and get back on track to mothering with as much intention and awareness as we can. In our darkest moments, we see that we are decent and worthy—even if our actions don't reflect this.

Despite my commitment to mindful mothering, I fall off the horse regularly (or the bull, as you'll read later on). After such an episode, I usually feel defensive. I wonder who wouldn't feel slightly crazed while attempting to answer an e-mail that requires more than the equivalent of a typed grunt, with three kids screaming in the background. In his book *After the Ecstasy, the Laundry*, Jack Kornfield quotes Pir Vilyat Khan, the head of the Sufi Order in the West. "Of so many great (spiritual) teachers I've met in India and Asia, if you were to bring them to America, get them a house, two cars, a spouse, three kids, a job, insurance, and taxes . . . they would all have a hard time." I don't include this quote to justify our lapses or meltdowns. But the next time you act in a way that doesn't reflect your commitment to mindful mothering, don't use your lapse as proof of your inadequacy. Don't let the slip steer you off course for more than the time it takes for you to collect yourself. Remind yourself that beyond the momentary hysteria lies a deep and thoughtful nature. *No matter what.*

· Tune the dial ·

Regardless of how effective, organized, or proactive we are, sometimes it seems as though we are barely keeping our heads above water. This was not always the case for me. All through school my classmates rolled their eyes when I raised my hand. I was the kind of person who liked to "just get a jump start on that paper" that was due in two months. In college, if you needed psychotically thorough notes after missing a class, I was your woman. Now I look at my house and wonder where that compulsively organized person went to, because we could use her around here. Books, backpacks, shoes, and toys are strewn everywhere. Children are half clothed and spottily washed. Unlike a research project, doing household chores (even when considerable attention is applied) just once doesn't do the trick. Teeth must be brushed multiple times daily. Laundry, like rust, never sleeps. At the end of the day I often feel as though I accomplished very little, very poorly.

In her 1988 study, Anne Wells found that mothers' ongoing self-esteem was considerably lower when they were with their children than in the company of other adults. The demands of mothering, including the lack of positive affirmation and feeling unable to competently manage our children's behavior, can contribute to temporary (or longer) feelings of inadequacy and discouragement.

This is the phenomenon that unfolded on Abby. For months Abby had been in a funk. She couldn't identify what exactly was bothering her, but she felt oppressed by the daily tedium of caring for her twin boys. Every morning she felt a slight twinge of dread knowing that she had to get through the entire day alone. When her husband tried to talk to her about her unhappiness, Abby cut him down at the knees with the simple though highly effective retort, "Why don't you try staying home for a while and giving this a shot. Then you might understand."

One night Abby put the boys in the tub only to return moments later and find the entire room submerged under two inches of water. No matter how many warnings she issued, the boys created mini-tsunamis night after night. The plaster in the living room was cracked and falling down from repeated soakings. Abby screamed at the boys until they began to cry. Then she dragged them out of the tub roughly. Thrusting pajamas over their heads, she put them in their room and slammed the door. After she stormed down the stairs she took a breath and wondered, "Is this who I have become? A shrill, impatient, constantly aggravated mother?" Later that night she admitted to her husband that she hated the way she felt about herself and toward the boys. Her husband pointed out that since she had the twins, she had given up a lot of the things that she loved doing—the things that connected her to that deeper, essential part of herself. Over the next few months Abby began meditating more regularly and took an art class. By intentionally creating time to realign with her core Self, Abby was able to tap into the restorative feelings she used to experience regularly.

Tune the dial is a reminder that underneath the static of our tension, stress, and annoyance is the clarity of the core Self. The core Self is like a radio station always sending a signal and waiting for us to tune in. As mothers, *tuning the dial* to the core Self is an essential survival technique. It is crucial to the emotional well-being of our children and ourselves. At the heart of Self is an unending source of patience, insight, wise instinct, expansiveness, and compassion. To the extent that we *tune the dial* and find ways to realign with our core Self, we gain access to the qualities that make us mindful mothers. Rather than view our mistakes as proof of our deficiency, the core Self allows us to use these lessons as stepping-stones to greater awareness. Moments of realigning to the Self are restorative, and we need it because a fourteen-hour day of hand-to-hand mothering usually is not. There are lots of ways to *tune the dial*: exercise, art, therapy, spiritual practice, being with close friends, gardening, hang gliding, alligator wrestling, whatever works. Most likely you already do know what to do to tune in; the trick is taking the time to do it.

· Just do it ·

One of the best ways to connect to the true Self or *tune the dial* is through meditation and other mindfulness practices. The Buddhist meditation master Sogyal Rinpoche writes: "It is meditation that slowly purifies the ordinary mind, unmasking and exhausting its habits and illusions, so that we can, at the right moment, recognize who we really are." Through meditation, we are able to momentarily quiet the thoughts, planning, judgments, wishes, and fears that often cloud our ability to tap into the core Self. Simply by sitting and focusing on our breath, we allow ourselves to gain access to a deeper, stiller, and more fundamental part of our beings. We get in touch with a peacefulness that the stress of mothering (and life) often conceals. The Dalai Lama writes, "One thing that meditation shows us is that the sense of peace already exists within us. We all have a deep desire for it even if it is often hidden, masked, thwarted."

Recently there has been a significant amount of scientific literature confirming the positive effects of meditation. In his book *Meditation for Dummies*, Stephan Bodian, former editor in chief of

Yoga Journal, summarizes these benefits. The physiological pay-offs include lower blood pressure, quicker recovery from stress, reduced serum cholesterol levels, reduction in the intensity of pain, and increased alpha rhythms—the brain waves associated with relaxation. He also points out some of the psychological benefits, such as increased empathy and reduction in acute and chronic anxiety. Another meta-analysis conducted by German researchers found that meditation practices were associated with significant reductions in depression, improved coping styles, and increases in measures of quality of life. Researchers such as Jon Kabat-Zinn, the founder of the Stress Reduction Clinic at the University of Massachusetts Medical Center, have known for years that meditation is one of the most effective and reliable ways to reduce the stress that complicates illness and jeopardizes our physical and emotional well-being. But the big question is, Is it powerful enough to reduce the stress associated with moth-ering? The answer is an unqualified yes.

Really, the best proof that meditation works comes from *just doing it.* Meditating is like lifting weights—you don't have to be-lieve it works, but if you work out every day, you'll see some convincing results.

The real challenge for most mothers is not believing that meditation will work but rather finding time to do it. Actually, you'll never find time to meditate; you have to make the time. Like the Nike commercial says, you have to *just do it.* This can be challenging, especially for mothers of young children. But if we are flexible and tenacious, we can *make* time to meditate. This might mean forgoing a bit of TV, or not making a phone call after the kids are asleep. It might mean meditating when people are napping or before everyone gets up. It may not be at the same time every day, but usually we can squeak twenty minutes out somewhere. I used to meditate between clients at my old job. (I also used to sleep at work on the floor with my door locked when I was pregnant, so maybe I'm not the best example of work etiquette.) If you are able, start off meditating for ten minutes a day. When you feel ready, try to extend your practice. The more consistently we meditate, the more we experience the benefits—like watching your child accidentally drag a rake along the side of your car with an equanimity you never knew you possessed.

I meditate because I am a different mother when I do. Meditation allows me to see my anger, frustration, or anxiety without getting consumed by it. I still feel my emotions, but they are less likely to overwhelm me and make me lash out. My fuse becomes longer. When I find myself coming up with a long list of reasons that I can't make time to do it, I come back with the mantra *just do it*. And I'm always glad I did.

THE INSTRUCTIONS ARE SIMPLE:

• • • • •

Sit down.

Close your eyes.

Sit in an upright position with your spine straight. Some people imagine that the head is like a balloon floating gently upward from the neck.

Remain still.

Keep your attention on your breath. As thoughts come into your mind (as they will), greet them with a "no big deal" attitude. Softly return your attention to the breath. Our minds are built with the "on" switch as the default setting. In order to pause them, we must be intentional about letting go of our natural tendency to plan, think, judge, and worry. Meditation is the pause button. It is a practice that invites us to take a twenty-minute (or however long) vacation from the constant flow of thoughts filling our minds. Perhaps you can follow your breath for three inhalations and exhalations only to find that on the fourth breath you are thinking about buying bacon. That's okay. As soon as you are aware that your mind has wandered, just return your focus to the breath. Let the thought of bacon drift off into the air like a passing cloud.

· Trust your gut ·

Perhaps the biggest bonus of regularly attuning to the authentic Self is benefiting from keener instincts. As mentioned many times before, the core Self is infinitely wise. Wise enough for anything that mothering can dish out. But at times we become separated from the benefit of this insight and clarity. We get mired in twisted thoughts or fears. We second-guess ourselves and make decisions that don't feel right at the time. Or perhaps we rationalize our shaky choices and hog-tie ourselves in them. In hindsight, we see the cracks in our logic.

Lynette's longtime babysitter, Ruth, moved suddenly when her husband got a job in another state. It was heart-wrenching for everyone. Ruth had been part of the family since the birth of Lynette's oldest daughter. Word of mouth yielded no good prospects for a replacement. Although she wasn't comfortable with the idea, Lynette advertised in the newspaper. The process wasn't a happy one. Each interview topped the previous one in absurdity. One woman called for the job but arrived with two other women (neither of whom spoke any English) for whom she was seeking employment. Another prospect arrived in stiletto heels, a miniskirt, and very, very long red nails. She also bore a striking resemblance to the actress Salma Hayek. Nice as she was, she did not seem as though she would adapt well to playing soccer and baseball in the muddy backyard with two school-age boys, although Lynette's teenage son lobbied heartily for her employment. This went on for two weeks and fourteen interviews until a woman showed up who looked fairly normal.

One of the questions that Lynette asked each participant was whether she had children. Ruth had brought along her daughter to work, and Lynette wanted to extend this offer to the new person. When asked, this babysitter said she and her husband did not have children yet. But upon calling her references, Lynette learned that she did in fact have a son who was living in another country with his grandmother. She called her friends and asked their opinions. Rather than *trusting her gut*, she started rationalizing because she was in a jam and needed someone to start as soon as possible. Lynette gave the woman the benefit of the doubt and hired her.

The second red flag went up when she called the woman's house to offer her the job. A man answered the phone and began swearing and screaming at the woman to pick up the receiver. Lynette's heart raced. There was a pause in the conversation, and all of Lynette's instincts sent out a unified directive: Hang up. Or politely tell her that you've found someone else. The core Self sent out its message. Lynette turned a deaf ear and asked the woman to start Monday.

Things went downhill from there. What followed was a string of tiny little signs leading to the inevitable end of the road.

Lynette soon learned that the woman had lied about being married and that she wasn't legally residing in the country. Finally, after the woman told a long and compelling story about how easy it is to kidnap children, Lynette pulled the plug. Only after, as she described it, "being bludgeoned over the head with a billboard spelling it out in black and white," Lynette decided to *trust her gut*. But not until she had put herself through two agonizing weeks of torture and self-doubt. On the woman's last day, Lynette made her husband stay home with the babysitter, feigning that he was working from home that day, just to keep an eye on her.

When we are really mindful and connected to the core Self, the right choices become available to us. This doesn't mean that the choices will necessarily be easy to determine. Sometimes we have to put the brakes on the *thinking* mind and let the *knowing* mind do the driving. Nor does it mean that *trusting your gut* will yield easy and comfortable outcomes. Sometimes our instincts ask us to go down a road where the right choice increases our pain, makes more work for us, or calls others to question our judgment. Seeking out treatment for a child experiencing emotional or behavioral problems may initially heighten the tension with that child and escalate his or her acting out. In the long run, however, the wise mind is able to see the rightness and logic of the choice. Our instincts, when informed by the core Self, rarely steer us wrong. As Jon Kabat-Zinn writes, "What is required to participate more fully in our own health and well-being is simply to listen more carefully and to trust what we hear, to trust the messages from our own life, from our own body and mind and feelings." In the long run, *trusting our gut* increases the likelihood we will make the right choices for ourselves and our children the first time around.

Chapter 16

. . .

The Eyes Have It:
Mothering in the World at Large

Each summer my grandparents would take their four children to a small church retreat in New Hampshire. The allure of the camp was a crystal clear lake where the kids could swim while the adults read and played cards on the beach. My grandparents lived in an urban blue-collar town where the closest thing they had to a lake was an iridescent marsh into which a neighboring factory dumped oily waste late at night. These summer excursions coin-

cided with the polio scares of the 1940s, and my grandmother
was rebuked and whispered about for letting her children swim
in potentially infested waters. (It is possible to catch polio from
swimming in proximity to others with the disease.) Despite this
social censure, she stuck to her guns and let her kids swim. She
had escaped a genocide; what was a little water? Even with the
knowledge that she was the subject of endless dining hall chatter,
she maintained an outgoing and warm attitude as she took her
seat at every meal. However, to my grandfather she would frequently whisper, *"Idle geese squawk loudest."* This mantra allowed
her to mother gracefully while placed under the microscope of
one hundred relatively idle vacationing women with close social
ties.

Mothering is hard enough to do when we're not being
judged and second-guessed. Typically, however, we aren't af-
forded much anonymity. On a daily basis we are asked to perform stressful and often unpleasant tasks in front of our families,
friends, and strangers. Imagine a heart surgeon being told that she
or he had to perform a precarious operation on the subway or in
a Pizza Hut. Strangers would be watching and offering their advice. "Oh, I wouldn't clamp the artery *there*! If you let that nurse
talk back to you like that, you're asking for a whole heap of trouble, lady." Often, mothering in public feels just like that.

Although the job of mothering will always be tough, the social aspect of mothering tends to intensify our feelings of inade-

quacy, anxiety, self-criticism, and anger. In real life, strangers wouldn't dream of going up to the surgeon and offering their judgments, criticisms, or a list of ways she could improve her performance. When someone does have a legitimate complaint, there's a formal review process to go through. Mothering, on the other hand, is an open invitation for just about anyone at any time to let us know what they think of how we're doing. Sometimes we can escape these unsought audiences. More often than not, we can't. By using some of the mantras in this section, it is possible to mother mindfully and seek refuge internally, no matter who's watching.

· Says who? ·

I can almost always pick out my friend Isabelle coming down the street in the middle of winter. No matter how cold it is, her children rarely have coats on. Isabelle has a lovely coat, which she wears at the first sign of a chill. While her children possess coats, they often choose not to partake in the comfort of these coats because they don't really *like* coats. Short of securing the coats to their bodies with duct tape, she was unable to get her children to keep the coats on their bodies. Usually, the coats were shed within fifteen minutes of a journey and left in various places throughout the city. Regardless of the temperature, they just didn't seem cold. I easily identify her flock, because in her wake a line of women forms (usually well-intentioned older grandmother types). These women either scream at her back or catch up to her and haul her aside in order to express their deep chagrin over her choice not to make her children wear coats. They usually point out the temperature (cold) as well as the possible outcomes of her decision (everything from runny noses to limb amputation from frostbite).

Isabelle tormented herself for a while regarding the coat issue. Was she being, as some suggested, a bad mother? How did other mothers get their children to don coats? She was bolstered when her pediatrician said there is no scientific evidence that being cold gives you a cold. And as she never locked them out of the apartment and on the street during cold snaps, the argument of death by exposure was invalidated. Isabelle decided to *trust her instincts* and left coat wearing to the discretion of her children.

Initially, the feedback she drew on the streets irritated her immensely. Early on, she would get defensive about the comments and either respond snidely or try to argue her circumstances (Look, I've tried to get these crazy kids to wear coats, but they're slippery little buggers!). Neither option worked well. Clearly, Isabelle had no control over what people said about her coatless children. She also had minimal control keeping the kids suited up in parkas. The only thing she could control was how she thought about the entire situation. According to *A Practitioner's Guide to*

Rational-Emotive Therapy, "cognition is the most important proximal determinant of human emotion." In short, what we tell ourselves about an event determines how we feel. Albert Ellis, founder of RET, asserts that our most distressing thoughts are centered around irrational beliefs. Often embedded within an irrational belief is a *should* or an *ought*. For example, in order for me to feel good about myself, people must approve of what I'm doing.

Early on when Isabelle met comments from the neighborhood help squad with the thought "Oh, these people think I'm a terrible mother who isn't taking care of her kids," she felt guilty and incompetent. Within that thought was the irrational belief that people *must* approve of her parenting choices in order for her to feel like a good mother. When she told herself, "These people have no right to comment on how I raise my kids. They *should* shut up," she felt irritated and defensive. The irrational belief buried in that thought was that in order for her to feel happy, people mustn't be bossy and interfering. This is not a good irrational thought if you live in New York City. Isabelle realized that in order for her to feel less reactive around her children's coat refusal and strangers' comments, she needed a mantra to transform her thoughts. Now every time a meddlesome bystander accosts her and tells her that her children should, ought to, have to, must, need to wear their coats, Isabelle repeats the mantra *says who?* She then civilly agrees that it *is* cold out and goes on her way.

Basically, *says who?* applies to all judgment calls in the gray (and sometimes not so gray) range. Anyone who has tried to raise a child knows that for every piece of expert advice, there is often an equally persuasive counterargument. As with highly complex tasks, there's no one right way to mother. Of course your child should not drink Drano (all the experts agree). But when an officious passerby tells you your one-year-old shouldn't have a pacifier or that your five-year-old mustn't play with dirty cans in the park, it's time for *says who?*

Says who? is a reminder that you are the ultimate authority. *Says who?* is a call to *trust your gut.* Of course guts will be wrong at times, but it's our choice. *Says who?* allows us to greet unsolicited and perhaps unwanted advice with composure and without reacting emotionally. This mantra helps us embrace the belief that others have every right in the world to offer advice, and we have every right in the world to ignore it. Rather than interpret this advice as proof we are haphazard mothers, we shrug it off with a "no big deal" attitude. "You don't like the fact that my child is wearing pajama bottoms instead of pants? That's fine." *Says who?* defuses these potentially distressing events in one fell swoop.

I've used this mantra many times on myself. After the birth of our third child, I was exhausted beyond anything I had ever felt. With the first two kids I followed a rigid bedtime routine. Woken children were soothed and settled back into their own beds. I waited out seemingly endless crying jags. But with the third, I wasn't willing to give up one second of repose. When he cried at night, he was quickly ushered into the comfort and haven of my bed. (Of course, this did little to encourage him to sleep through the night.) Each time the thought "He really shouldn't be in your bed" came up, it was instantly met with the retort "*Says who?*" My gut told me that the baby in the bed was what worked for me under these circumstances, no matter what any facts, data, or anecdotal evidence offered. Eventually, he started sleeping through the night in his own bed. But for those intervening months, the mantra *says who?* gave me the reinforcement I needed to listen to my instincts.

Am I reading this right?

It's one thing to take affront when a parent, a friend, or a stranger openly criticizes our mothering. But sometimes we think there is judgment where there is not. Sometimes the negative scripts we run in our heads—often without our being aware of them—cause us to distort reality. It can be like wearing the opposite of rose-colored glasses—lenses that make things look worse than they really are. Cognitive psychologists such as Kenneth Dodge use the term "attributional bias" to refer to our tendency to distort actual events in our environment so that they match our beliefs about how the world works. In his work, Dodge found that aggressive kids interpreted ambiguous interpersonal cues as aggressive, whereas nonaggressive children saw the same exchange as bearing no threat. In short, we see what we expect to see or sometimes what we fear is true.

Oftentimes, these illogical beliefs have a logical origin. If we come from very critical families, we might possess a general expectation that people will respond critically to us because in the past this has been true. The problem is that we carry these expectations around as we interact with others in the world. We anticipate that they will treat us in a similar fashion. In fact, we may experience others as more disparaging than they really are. And because of our interpretation of these events, we may even become upset or irritated by a fairly benign interpersonal exchange. The power of the mantra *am I reading this right?* is that it helps us step out of our reactive patterns and question what is really going on in the present moment. Rather than assuming people are being judgmental and harsh, we give ourselves the option of rereading a situation. *Am I reading this right?* safeguards us against being overly sensitive to perceived put-downs—particularly when the only threat is in our own minds. This process opens up a wider range of thoughts, feelings, and behaviors. Using this mantra helps us *rewire* the way we look at the world.

My friend Anne recently had the following encounter at the library. Before continuing, I must confess that I belong to a subgroup of mothers for whom nothing provokes as much stress as does a visit to the public library. It has often been a wonder to me how a children's library could be one of the worst places you could possibly take your young children. Mine have a long history of emptying shelves in the blink of an eye and shunning the librarian's pleas for them to lower their voices. Heightening this tension is the fact that our town's children's library has a very appealing reading perch that children are banned from until they are six. This requires me to spend the entire visit prying my two-year-old off the structure by his ankles as he waves suspended like a sail from the top rail. As we drive by the library now, my children ask longingly when we can return. The reply is always the same, "In four years, when your brother can sit in the perch."

The day Anne was there, she saw a woman having a hard time controlling her two young children, whom she described as "obstreperous, but very cute." Anne was at a computer terminal reading a humorous e-mail her friend had sent her and laughing. As the woman was leaving, she leaned over Anne and said in a hurt and angry voice, "I saw you laughing at me because my kids were out of control. That wasn't very nice of you." Anne, being the kindest person I know, felt horrible and pleaded that she wasn't making fun of her. In fact, she had just been thinking how adorable they were. But the woman didn't believe her. In the woman's mind, she was unable to manage her children's behavior in the library, which meant that she was an inadequate mother, and Anne *must* be laughing at her. Anne's laughter confirmed the woman's inner dialogue and verified her darkest fears about her ineptitude. (These are the times you want to put your arms around a desperate mother and say, "It's not you, my friend: the library is a setup. You've been suckered in by the whole 'family friendly' myth.")

The woman's distress hinged on a few of the irrational beliefs that many of us experience. First, we believe that in order to prove we are good mothers, we must always be in control of our kids' behavior. This would be a fine assumption if mothering did not bear such a resemblance to herding cats. Surely well-behaved children make our job easier, but controlling our children's behavior is not always an option. Nor is it necessarily beneficial. Buddhist teacher Jack Kornfield writes about the perils of attempting to micromanage our children: "Yes, we can love and care for them, but if we try to control them, we only create suffering." Suffering for mothers, surely.

The second "thinking error" the woman in the library made was assuming that Anne was laughing at her. We've all done this. Unfortunately, misconstruing others' behavior only serves to heighten our stress and emotional discomfort. What we need in this instance is a mantra to check in with reality.

Am I reading this right? is a mantra designed to rectify some of the "situation-reading" errors we all make. *Am I reading this right?* is a cue to question our beliefs or fears that we are being mocked, laughed at, disparaged, or judged. There are two steps to this disputation. The first is to ask if you are positive that you're reading the situation correctly. Just this simple question can often clear up misconceptions about people's intentions. Sometimes it helps to entertain alternative possibilities for another's behavior. In the case with Anne, the mother might have seen Anne reading and told herself that Anne was probably laughing at a joke.

We often teach high-risk kids to attribute rude or inconsiderate behavior to the fact that they might be having a bad day—or experiencing some other negative state or feeling. In short, this type of attribution shifts things from being about us to being about something outside of us. In this way we train our minds to give the world the benefit of the doubt. The attributions we make regarding another's thoughts and behaviors toward us instantly become more benign. The second step of *am I reading this right?* asks us to assume the worst is true. If you really are being judged, gently remind yourself that in the bigger scheme of things it doesn't matter; it's not your problem. You don't need the world's affirmation to feel like a competent mother. Take a moment to focus inward. Breathe deeply and let any accumulating stress be released. Finally, remind yourself that praise from others is nice but not necessary to know that you're doing the job well.

⸙ Find your inner mole ⸙

Of all the public mothering moves I most admire, Amy's ability to act like she's mothering in complete and total isolation ranks highest. About two years ago, Amy was in the stage of her mothering career when she had more children under the age of five than is recommended for your emotional and physical well-being. Despite the warning labels her husband pasted on their foreheads, Amy frequently left the apartment and took her children out in public. As with any brood, hers would occasionally hit critical mass. The ice cream truck would come and Amy might decide that it was too close to dinner for a fudge pop. This often precipitated children hurling themselves to the ground. Or it would be time to go home and they would cling to the swing as if they were about to be thrown into a bonfire. Not quite ready for pool time to be over? Children would scatter like mice until she was forced to fish them out from under the cabana chairs where they had burrowed.

In the midst of all this commotion, Amy would adopt a beatific half smile even as she was carrying two toddlers on her hips like potato sacks. Whatever consequences or plan of action she decided on, she stuck with it. She rarely bent her will to *avoid a scene*. I asked her how she was able to remain so calm when chaos had broken loose. How was it that she found the conviction to stick to her guns when it would have been easier to give them the damn ice cream and avoid the public disturbance? Amy replied that after her fourth child, she just started pretending that no one could see her. "I'm like a mole working underground."

Webster's dictionary describes a mole as "one who works in the dark." Think of it however you want—dimming the lights, turning inward, pretending you're invisible, blocking out the noise—the end results are the same. *Finding your inner mole* allows us to remain goal directed, tuned to our instincts, and resilient against the stares and comments of others. It liberates us. *Finding your inner mole* is a reminder that we can't control who might be watching us (or perhaps even judging us), but we can control how much we focus on our audience. Tempting as it may be to alter our mothering to avoid a scene, it may not be in the best interest of our child. In fact, often it is not. Following through on limits is a powerful mothering tool, even though the fallout is not always pretty. *Finding your inner mole* helps focus your attention away from the stress onlookers can cause back toward the task of mothering.

Take to the stage

There can be downsides to mothering in places where other people can actually *see you* like the ones mentioned in the previous mantras. They include the negative feelings associated with being judged, second-guessed, and accosted by strangers. But there's an upside, too. Typically, we modulate our emotions and behaviors when we are being watched far more than we do when we think we are alone. Social psychologists have labeled this phenomenon self-presentation theory. We have a natural drive to want to look good in front of others. We are hardwired to want others to think highly of us. Because of this, we often put our best foot forward in public. We alter many of our impulses and tone down behavior that we know isn't socially acceptable.

A few weeks ago my father-in-law was staying with us. His flight was delayed because of bad weather, so he was in the position of observing a school morning in our home. I have stayed overnight at the houses of other people who have children, so I know it is possible for a morning routine to flow smoothly and peacefully. I have friends whose children wake happily, put on clothing, brush their teeth, eat breakfast, collect their belongings, and catch the bus. This is not what happens most mornings at our house. Nevertheless, I attempted desperately to sell this image to my father-in-law. Watching his face as I hustled his grandchildren through the post-waking paces was like watching a person whose new car won't start. At first he had a benign and hopeful look. This turned into concern. Slowly, irritation creased his brow. My father-in-law is a very polite man, so he said little during these shenanigans. On several occasions he chuckled with a "children will be children" laugh. But I knew that secretly he was thinking, "My God! She's raised my grandchildren as wild animals."

That morning I felt as if I were onstage with the spotlight shining directly down on me. The interesting aspect of this experience was that having him observe my every move kept me on the straight and narrow. I know from experience that yelling and screaming does nothing to facilitate getting kids out the door, yet often I find myself shrieking, *"Get dressed now or I will beat you soundly!!!!"* Yet being watched made me the voice of reason. He may not have given me extra style points for my performance, but I did. In fact, I was greatly pleased with my restraint and dignity. My composure also seemed to shift the mood in favor of a saner morning.

Now when I feel as though I might come unglued and do or say something detrimental to my kids in a moment of distress, I use the mantra *take to the stage*. It's important to clarify a few aspects of this mantra. The purpose of the mantra is not to impress onlookers. You're not acting or performing for the benefit of someone else; you're imagining an audience for your *own benefit*. Nor is *take to the stage* meant to overemphasize the outcome of the event. If you lose your composure in the final act, consider it a dress rehearsal. *Take to the stage* is really just a call to act as though your beloved and gentle aunt were in the audience watching you handle a tough situation. She would understand if you lost your cool, but you'd rather not do it in front of her. *Take to the stage* lets us tap into that same level of control and self-monitoring we have in front of others even when we're alone. *Take to the stage* is a cue to rally your resources to deliver a performance that is effective and often beyond what you thought you had in you.

· Nice move ·

Just as we are naturally drawn to comparing our children to other children, comparisons between ourselves and other mothers invariably arise. It's part of how we are built. We learn by watching. And given the fact that there is no mothering manual, the powers of observation and comparison offer us invaluable tools for learning. Sometimes even people we aren't that crazy about have some amazing mothering moves. This is what happened to my friend Paula and me. When our sons were about two years old, Paula and I met Abigail. Abigail is the type of person who is quite pleasant but has the knack of making you feel incompetent after about fifteen minutes of making her acquaintance. "Kix cereal? Never heard of it," she says, whipping out the organic equivalent. "Oh, we don't have any plastic toys in our home [unbeknownst to us, they leech some neurotoxic chemical] and certainly nothing electronic." Abigail spent hours reading to her child every day. Her daughter could offer up a cogent explanation of what a double helix was by the time she was five years old.

But the kicker was when she came over to Paula's house and asked her to please turn off the television because her child had never been "exposed." For those of you who don't allow TV into your home, you are my heroes. I wish I had the moral fortitude to be like you, but I do not. I have created many elaborate rationalizations as to why I allow TV. We have employed sentences from "We need to teach them how to *moderate* their watching" to "They won't understand their peer group without TV." But the real reason is that it makes them be quiet when it's on.

Although we secretly resented Abigail lording her excellent mothering over us, we began to notice that she really was an *excellent* mother. The thing that Paula and I noticed most was that she talked endlessly to her child. Not chatter, but real conversations. She took pains to explain things, ask questions, and provide examples. Rather than the conversation killer "just cuz," which I often offered in response to my child's queries, Abigail expounded. As we listened to her, we often raised our eyebrows in silent appreciation. *Nice move* is a mantra designed to acknowledge the mindful mothering of others, even when these moves come from unlikely or even irritating sources. In doing so, we open up the possibility of working these behaviors, attitudes, or approaches into our own mothering repertoires.

I have watched friends calmly deal with situations that would have resulted in my becoming apoplectic. I would mentally tuck these maneuvers away. The next time I came up against a similar battle, I took a deep breath, recalled their *nice move*, and tried to follow their model (albeit with varying success). *Nice move* can impact our mothering in subtle ways as well. Recently, I was about to give my son the brush-off after the twentieth question about ducks when I remembered Abigail's *nice move* and took the time to really respond to him. Think of *nice move* as the owner's manual you never had. Say it out loud and you've just given a fellow mom a boost that is rare in this line of work.

Chapter 17

. . .

Mantras for the Working Mom

I don't consider myself to be a person prone to feelings of unjustified guilt. If you are my friend (or mother, sister, or husband), I will forget your birthday every year and not beat myself up about it too much. But, as most of us know, no one is getting out of mothering without spending quite a bit of time wearing the self-imposed hair shirt. To greater and lesser degrees we feel guilt and regret for a multitude of situations. Some big, some small. We feel guilty for getting divorced, for missing the soccer game (again), for giving our kids hot dogs four nights in a row, for paying more attention to one child, for just about everything. But nobody knows guilt like the working mother.

In fact, being a working mother offers opportunities for all types of intense emotions: stress, fatigue, and occasionally elation when it all comes together. In the end, what it boils down to is that working mothers work a lot. There are never-ending demands on our time and energy. It often feels like we are doing fifty things at once. The stress of being harried is magnified by the sneaking suspicion we're doing a half-baked job across the board. Sometimes I look accusingly at the fading sun as though it were a timer about to ring. "Okay, class, pencils down. Please hand in your papers." "But I need more *time*," I think, panic-stricken. The mantras in this chapter can't lengthen your day or clone you. But they can help us weed out the nonessentials that creep into the life of working mothers, and gain some clarity when dealing with the rest.

Give up the guilt

The first time I heard someone come out and say *it* I was shocked, though giddy and enormously relieved. I had been talking to my supervisor, a woman I respected greatly, about balancing a family and an often stressful career. At the end of the conversation she said, "I couldn't not work. There is no way I could sit on the floor all day and roll a ball around. I'm just not cut out for it. Two days a week? Fine. But seven? No way. I'd go nuts playing with my kids all day." Did she just say that? I quickly looked at the open door to see if she'd been overheard. I felt the urge to protect her from her heresy. Isn't that tantamount to "I don't really like being a mother all that much?" I mean, we're child psychologists. We make our livings spending our days with other people's kids. Aren't we supposed to want to make mud cakes with our own offspring? For a lot of mothers (not just psychologists), the answer is "ideally, yes; but actually, no."

We work for many different reasons. Many of us find employment outside of the home because we enjoy eating, wearing clothes, and not being homeless. Most of us work because we have to work. Some of us work because we love what we do. Unless we have a really tough job with extreme stress or horrendous working conditions, work offers some great perks. Here I'm referring to the social, emotional, and sometimes intellectual payoffs. Work often provides complex challenges, which can promote a sense of mastery and heightened esteem. We get to hang around people who use utensils when they eat and have seen PG-13 movies. You might even go shopping with a coworker during a lunch break without screaming at her to get out from under the clothes rack. If you have a certain type of job, you might travel for a night or two during the year, get room service, watch the television show of your choice, and sleep un-interrupted for eight solid hours. My friend who works on the phones all day puts up with the irate and cranky customers to be able to carry on adult conversations. Commuting all of a sudden seems blissful compared to the mayhem that was left behind.

Unfortunately, woven into the mix is the guilt that working mothers often feel. Because I work, I rarely chaperone field trips. I feel bad leaving my children at home with our sitter when they are sick. When I left my first son in day care while I finished my last year of clinical training, I experienced guilt of epic propor-tions. However, guilt comes in many varieties, and not all guilt should be treated equally. Sometimes guilt is a sign that some-thing is out of whack. Vicky has her own architecture firm. It's usually feast or famine. When things are busy, many of her moth-ering duties are pushed to the back burner. As she drifts off to sleep at night, she notices she feels higher doses of mother guilt as a result of her schedule. "But it makes sense," she told me. "I guess the guilt is just confirming to me that things aren't in bal-ance—that I'm working too much to keep all the balls in the air. It's a signal to cut back. Usually, things sort themselves out and I go through a dry spell when I'm home a lot. If not, the guilt sometimes helps me say 'no' to the next job. The one that would have created total havoc."

Other times, guilt stems from a deeper place. Perhaps we feel guilty because we really would rather be at work than playing in the sandbox with our kids. Or we feel guilty that we're happier, more satisfied, and at our best at work as opposed to home. Or guilty that our stomach sinks and we contemplate turning tail and running upon hearing chaos on the other side of the door when we return home. By the way, if this is true, you're not alone. One study found that the lowest emotional point in a working mother's day was dinnertime. Her highest was around eleven-thirty A.M., when she was at work. This is where the mantra *give up the guilt* comes in. Rather than beating myself up by the feeling, I gently remind myself to *give up the guilt*. Stewing in guilt is not going to change anything. I'm still going to work. It doesn't make me a more mindful or present mother. It just takes a good knock at my self-esteem. I remind myself of all the scientific literature that attests to the fact that the children of working moms do just fine. Whenever my guilt surfaces around these types of emotionally charged issues, those that aren't negotiable, I remind myself to *give up the guilt* and move on.

· Flip the switch ·

It is eight o'clock on Monday morning. Now it is eight-ten. Oh look, eight-fifteen. The mental limit I have set is eight-twenty. Okay, I *dare* the Universe to make her more than thirty minutes late. I am standing at the door pacing because it is now eight-thirty-five and our babysitter is stuck in traffic. I go so far as to tap my watch because maybe the digital read isn't correct. I think ahead to the five graduate students standing at the door waiting for me to open the clinic. Now I picture their clients slowly ambling up, seeing that the clinic is still locked, and drifting back into the crowded halls of the high school where the clinic is based. I think of the speech my boss could give me, since this is not the first (or tenth) time this has happened. Now my kids catch the drift that I'm still in the apartment when I should be gone. This is their cue to cling like beggar's lice to my legs so that I won't leave. Crying begins. Instantaneously, my anger is turned against my husband, who *did not* have to wait at home for the babysitter to arrive before he caught his bus into the city. He's probably reading the paper now and not truly appreciating the civility of his circumstances.

Finally she arrives, panting and apologetic. I continue my pacing down at the bus stop. Judging from the glances I am getting, I must look either drug-addled or insane. This is my hint that I need to *flip the switch*. *Flipping the switch* simply means stepping out of the cascading flow of negative thoughts threatening to pull me under. *Flipping the switch* is my cue to gently but firmly pull myself out of the swamp I'm sinking into. I take a few deep breaths. Just like that, I begin to quiet my mind and pay attention to my body. I reel in my racing thoughts. I stop catastrophizing the entire morning away. I tell myself I will get to work, slightly late but in one piece. The morning will unfold, though perhaps not as smoothly as I'd like. No one will die. Feelings of irritation from those waiting for me will dissipate by lunch. I remind myself that these are the perils of the working mother. We all have them. My troubles are not unique, unusual, or worse than any one else's. *By flipping the switch*, I pull myself out of the spiral of negative thoughts and feelings that works like the domino effect to knock me down for the rest of the day. *Flipping the switch* creates the intention to come back to center.

You might say to yourself, "Well, it's not so easy to do a mental one-hundred-eighty-degree turn when it feels like everything is crashing down on me." That's a good point. *Flipping the switch* can feel strange at first. We aren't used to giving up our anger and frustration so abruptly. A deeper part of us may want someone to recognize how incredibly hard this juggling act can be. It is difficult—unbelievably difficult. If you need to be angry about it, that's fair, too. But working mothers don't need any energy drains. And getting locked into these types of negative emotional spirals will deplete us quickly. I've heard mothers say that starting the day off with car pool, babysitter, school, or a sick kid crisis sets the tone for the whole day. But *flip the switch* offers a way out. The more we can practice this process (and being a working mother gives us plenty of opportunity), the easier it will be to *flip the switch* when we need it most.

· Cut the suckers ·

How thin can you stretch a working mother? So thin you can see through her. Jennifer is a special education teacher. On a typical day she leaves the house at seven-thirty A.M. and returns home by four-thirty P.M. Her afternoons usually consist of helping children with homework and then carting them around to more lessons than the progeny of British royalty attend. After going to swimming, piano, soccer, and gymnastics in one day, she confessed she hadn't realized it had gotten so out of control until she set the odometer and realized that in one afternoon she had driven seventy-five miles for extracurricular activities. On top of that, she was the type of person who insisted on actually cleaning her house on a regular basis. Jennifer looked exhausted because she was exhausted.

This spring our trees looked depleted, too. At our behest, our neighbor came down and explained how we are slowly draining the life out of our trees by not cutting off the sucker branches. He patiently explained to us transplanted city dwellers that the fruit trees won't flower because they have been taken over by suckers—offshoots that draw all of the energy out of the tree. In a sense, many of the extraneous activities in our lives are like sucker branches. They pop up unnoticed at first. Soon, however, they threaten to overrun the tree. Unless they are controlled, they sap our resources until we are nothing but fruitless, flowerless, desiccated trunks. *Cut the suckers* is a mantra that asks us to bring awareness to what is essential in our lives. It encourages us to cultivate what we need and snip off the rest. *Cut the suckers* is a signal, particularly for working mothers with limited time, to resist the tendency to fill up every moment of our lives with action. Buddhist teacher Sogyal Rinpoche writes: "If we look into our lives, we will see clearly how many unimportant tasks, so called 'responsibilities' accumulate to fill them up . . . We tell ourselves that we want to spend time on the important things of life, but there never *is* any time." The mantra isn't a call to live like a monk or refuse our children cultural exposure, but it is a call to be intentional about what we take on. In doing so, we increase our chances of thriving or at least maintaining some semblance of sanity.

Chapter 18

• • •

Staying at Home

After Megan had her first baby, she took a temporary leave from her job and stayed home. In the back of her mind, she entertained thoughts of not going back to work, but she wanted to keep her options open while she got the lay of the land. What she found was rocky terrain and the feeling that she was constantly on the verge of losing her footing. Megan loved her baby dearly but decided after a year that she would return to work. She told people it was because of finances. But in truth she was blindsided by how difficult staying at home really was. "I don't know what I thought it would be like," she said. "But I'll tell you one thing. In my blissful fantasy it wasn't that . . . hard."

When Megan had her second child she did another stay-at-home trial run. She mentally geared up, entertaining hopes that with her beefed-up baby experience she'd be like a duck in water. Maybe the first time she was just caught off guard. She was back at her desk three months later. After her third child Megan dove in to stay-at-home mothering headfirst, and there she stays. She would go back to work, she confided, but it's too hard to get out the door every morning.

In my mind, there's nothing more rewarding, worthwhile, and spiritually growth-inducing than staying home with your children. But let's face it: it's no cakewalk. Many refer to parenting as a calling. In that context, stay-at-home mothers are the high priestesses of the movement. The following mantras are designed to help us recognize and value the significance of what we do, much of which is unnoticed or taken for granted. They encourage us to bring a revitalized energy and open mind to our task on a daily basis.

· Find a herd ·

It may have come to your attention that mothering is often a solitary process. Actually, it can generate a loneliness of existential proportions. This is especially true if you are the first of your friends to take the plunge. When I had my son, my friends were most definitely not in the same frame of mind. One friend actually panicked. "Oh no! What are you going to do?" Why this came as a surprise, I'm not sure. I had been married for five years. It's unclear how much longer they thought it would be prudent to wait. But this situation left me basically alone with a baby. A lovely boy, but prone to screaming his head off relentlessly in an apartment the size of an ice cream truck.

As many young mothers do in New York City, I took to the streets. The problem was that I didn't know anyone with kids. I decided to take matters into my own hands. Each day regardless of the weather, I would plant myself opportunistically on a park bench with the plan of breaking into conversation at an appropriate juncture. I would give compliments to other mothers' children so they would take a liking to us. I harbored transparent hopes that they would want to spend hours hanging out with us (preferably in their apartment because ours was too small). I had lots of snacks (kosher, vegetarian, nut-free) to strategically offer mothers of wailing children—after checking for food allergies. I knew my internal level of desperation for company, but I didn't know what it looked like to outside observers until my husband watched me one evening from across the street.

My target that afternoon had been a babysitter caring for a child about my son's age. She expressed the same tolerance level for me that she did for the baby—she was patient, but this wasn't her destination of choice. After about twenty minutes of spying, my husband walked over to us with a concerned look on his face. He was like the guy in a movie who finds a passport hidden in his wife's underwear drawer with her face but a different name. *Who is this woman I married?* He pulled me aside. "Honey, are you stalking that woman?" I assured him that I didn't know what he was talking about. "I've been watching you and you've been following her around the park like a neglected poodle. I don't really think she's that interested in *being your friend*. Is this what you do every day?" "No," I replied indignantly as I rattled the baby carrot sticks I had been about to ply her with.

After some effort and time, I found friends. Good friends, my herd. As an aside, I hope using the term "herd" is not offensive. (Don't think goats; think wild, beautiful mustangs on the range.) Typically, people and animals don't go off into the wilderness when they most need help or are vulnerable. We rely on social networks to create a sense of safety, belonging, and security. Yet after having a baby, just when we could most benefit from the support of others, we often find ourselves completely alone. At least I did. Not just physically alone, but emotionally marooned.

There are times when mothering young children will feel lonely. It's just part of the deal. But *finding a herd* can transform the emotional valence of our mothering experience. *Finding a herd* mitigates the alienation we often feel. These friends would eat with us when our partners were working late. They would sit for endless hours on the living room floor in the dead of winter when we couldn't go outside. But mostly what they did was make me feel like I really hadn't fallen into a black hole. The feelings of guilt, boredom, stress, and confusion that I often thought would consume me dissipated after being with others going through the exact same things. As therapists, one of the most powerful tools we enlist is normalizing people's feelings in response to an unpleasant event. Knowing that someone else felt like she was on the brink of madness after another sleepless night made me feel like I wasn't alone.

Lest you think I'm referring to a large throng of people, a herd can be as little as two or as many as you can shoehorn into your home. And no two members of the herd even need to know each other. They needn't have much in common except finding themselves in the possession of a child. In fact, once we stood back and looked objectively at our herd, we were shocked at how different we really were. It didn't matter, though. We were blood sisters out of the deep need not to be alone in all this. We became compatible for the sake of companionship. The only steadfast rule of thumb I stick to is that all herd members should be as nonjudgmental as possible. Mothering is hard enough without being put down by your pack.

· Find flow ·

If you have chosen to stay home rather than work outside the home, many mundane tasks may fall under your jurisdiction of duties. But like most things (or all things), how we experience those activities is largely driven by how we choose to see them. Thich Nhat Hahn, the Buddhist monk, writes: "To my mind, the idea that doing dishes is unpleasant can occur only when you aren't doing them. Once you are standing in front of the sink with your sleeves rolled up and your hands in the warm water, it is really quite pleasant." I am currently lobbying for Thich to leave his monastery in France, live with us, and just start pitching in around here.

One way to transform our experience of almost any activity is by achieving a deep engagement in what we are doing. Some people call this "flow"—a heightened state of focused awareness (not unlike meditation) during which the mind is totally absorbed in the present moment. Mihaly Csikszentmihalyi, author of *Flow: The Psychology of Optimal Experience*, defines it as the "state in which people are so involved in an activity that nothing else seems to matter." I have always been a runner. And through running I find that I'm able to achieve this type of focused attention. I get completely absorbed in what's going on at that moment. I feel my feet hitting the ground, a series of unfortunate cramps in my side, my breath change as the hills get steeper, and my heart rate slow as I cool down.

Flow can be achieved in many ways: through sports, artistic expression, engaging work, and spiritual practices. Even aspects of mothering can help us find flow. When I was pushing 120 pounds of kids in that stroller up the hill in August, I also felt flow. The outside world faded away, including my hunger, the trucks, the sirens, the objections of my passengers. Perhaps you find yourself wondering whether pushing a stroller up a hill produces the same kind of flow that the complicated work of a surgeon, editor, or pilot does. The answer seems to be, it depends on the way you decide to see it. In the book *Divergent Realities: The Emotional Lives of Mothers, Fathers, and Adolescents*, the authors write that the tasks inherent in mothering and housekeeping represent a kind of "anti-flow." They cite various authors who label these tasks as mind-numbing, vacant, repetitive, and boring. On the surface, this seems logical. If we consider them aversive, our natural inclination will be resistance rather than immersion, a mind-set that would thwart achieving flow.

Yet Csikszentmihalyi describes workers involved in what many would consider menial activities finding flow. He writes that these workers achieved this state by "allowing themselves to be lost in the interaction so that their selves could emerge stronger afterward." In fact, these workers became so engrossed in these mundane tasks that many identified them as being as

pleasurable as leisure activities. Eastern thinkers have a phenomenon similar to flow, which they call Yu. As Csikszentmihalyi
points out, one main difference exists between Yu and flow. Unlike flow, which is typically heightened by novel and challenging
circumstances, the process of Yu "disregards objective conditions
entirely in favor of spiritual playfulness and transcendence of ac-
tuality." Whether the external conditions of the task are boring
becomes irrelevant with Yu. So, when it comes to some of the
more supposedly mundane tasks of mothering and housework,
perhaps what I'm really trying to say is *find Yu.*

The point here is not to make you feel guilty if you don't *find
flow* scrubbing the bathtub. I don't like housework, but on the
rare occasions I do it, I try to immerse myself in it as a means of
self-protection. (It may be more difficult to *find flow* when a toddler is pulling on your clothing or clinging to your leg, but just
think of it as a momentary distraction.) As with many mantras in
this book, *find flow* is a call to find an abiding peacefulness, not
by changing the environment but by transcending our typical
way of interacting with it. Next time you find yourself resisting
the laundry, see if it's possible to *find flow (or Yu).* If not, have a
beer and go dancing.

· No task more supreme ·

Lisa had a J.D. and an M.B.A. by the time she was twenty-six years old and worked in a prestigious law firm as an environmental advocate. She was on track to becoming a partner when she and her husband decided to start a family. After the birth of her first child, Lisa stopped working cold turkey. After quitting, she felt liberated by the flexibility of her schedule and not having to write down her billable time every six minutes. Lisa loved staying home with her first baby. By the second one, however, cute as he was, Lisa started getting the itch to be back in the workplace. She had always been a highly goal-directed, achievement-focused person, and leaving the work arena caused her to feel like she'd been left in the dust. Initially, every time she spoke to one of her friends who continued her career after having a family, Lisa felt pangs of uncertainty about her choice to jump ship. But when she stood back and reflected on the situation, Lisa knew in her gut that she made the right decision.

Lisa admitted that a significant amount of her longing to return to work came from being conditioned to connect her sense of identity with her achievements. Until she quit her job, Lisa was unaware how much her accomplishments provided an unspoken validation of her intelligence, success, and ultimately her worth. Leaving all that external validation behind caused her to question who she really was. Anyone leaving a highly rewarding job where praise is flung around freely and feelings of accomplishment are enjoyed regularly should be put in a decompression chamber before becoming a stay-at-home mother. No one would argue about the intrinsic rewards and joy that come with raising children. However, saving the tundra from arctic drilling, managing a busy office, being a successful salesperson, or putting out fires and getting a paycheck for your efforts offers a steady flow of ego enhancement.

For some, becoming a stay-at-home mother means abandoning a role that we have spent most of our lives trying to construct. Lisa felt naked without her work identity. It took her some time to see that her job at home with her children was just as worthy and valid as her role as a lawyer. Each time her insecurities were triggered, Lisa reminded herself that there is *no task more supreme* than raising sentient beings. Whenever coworkers made comments about how much she had sacrificed for her family by giving up her career, Lisa reminded herself that there is no task more supreme than hers. Use this mantra with every bowl of macaroni served. The mantra *no task more supreme* reaffirms that staying at home, while often not as outwardly validating as the workplace can be, is as big a mission. We've been highly trained to think otherwise, so use this mantra in full force. Each time you think your worth was more evident before you made the choice to stay at home, use *no task more supreme* to think again.

Note: There is a note of caution to this mantra. One of the traps that Lisa felt she fell into from time to time was her belief that the sacrifice she made should somehow manifest itself in her children. She admitted in frustration after her oldest began having trouble in school, "I felt that I had given up my career to stay home and I always felt like they should have an edge somehow on working mothers' kids. More secure, more independent, smarter. I don't know—there should be some proof to make me feel like I hadn't done this for nothing."

Each time we find ourselves projecting these needs onto our children, it is an opportunity to once again see that *they are who they are*. Unless our child has unique emotional or physical needs that require our individual care, chances are he or she will do just as well whether we work or not. Using the mantra *no task more supreme* is a reminder that the choice to stay home is valid and should be made because it's what *we* want to do, not because we expect to see payoffs in our kids' achievements.

· It's in there ·

Grace is a very talented artist who waited until the last minute to have children. Although she loves her kids fiercely, she mourns the freedom and creative aspects of her life she surrendered to start a family. She still works on her art when she can, but it's tough to be a full-time mom of young children and an artist. In fact, when she does have time to paint, she frequently finds herself staring at the canvas and thinking that what she'd really like to do is take a nap. "Being a mother has sucked every ounce of creativity from my body," she told her husband.

A poet I know said she didn't write one word when her kids were small. Being so focused on satisfying the physical and emotional demands of young children leaves very little left over for artistic pursuits. She reassured herself that her urge to write would return by using the mantra *it's in there*. Rather than visualizing her art as a boat that had sailed, leaving her alone on the shore with tiny, hungry cannibals, she saw it as a seed that was lying dormant. With the proper conditions, it would bloom. This goes for hobbies, reading for pleasure, or urges to do anything but watch movies (if you can stay awake). When you wonder where your desire to learn Italian went, remind yourself *it's in there*. When you have more than four hours of uninterrupted sleep a night and have time to think of things other than diapers, choking hazards, and the lyrics of "Yankee Doodle," who can tell what might spring out of you?

Chapter 19

. . .

Asking for Help

For many of us, asking for help does not come naturally. When I need to ask for a friend to watch my kids or pick them up from school, I preface it with "I'm so sorry to ask, but . . ." Why am I so sorry? I wouldn't flinch if someone asked me to help. Sometimes, despite all of the rational thoughts telling me otherwise, asking for help makes me feel as though I have failed. There's a chink in the armor. We come from a highly individualistic culture that celebrates autonomy, independence, and self-sufficiency.

Unfortunately, those characteristics are not conducive to mothering while maintaining your mental health.

Mothering, in fact, is best done *interdependently*—as mentioned before, preferably in some kind of a herd. The other day, there were three adults actively taking care of my three kids. I was standing at the sink thinking, "This is the perfect ratio." Then I wondered how I do it alone. How does anyone? A good friend lamented to me that since I moved away, she doesn't have anyone she can call up and hand her three kids off to when she needs a few hours to get things done. Her mission was clear. "It's sad, but you'll have to be replaced. Pronto." The mantras in this section are reminders to look for help, ask for help, and take the help whenever and wherever offered (even when not offered). The more we ask for, the more we get. And the more we get, the better off we are.

· Grab an end ·

Last week my mother asked me to move a picnic table for her. In terms of picnic tables, it's a monster. I stood around drinking iced tea, reflecting on its size and heft while waiting for my husband to come outside. As soon as he arrived, I asked him to *grab an end*. Not once as I was considering moving the picnic table did I entertain the idea of transporting it myself. In fact, the first thought that crossed my mind was maybe I could locate a cousin to replace me entirely. Reducing my load to the point of becoming an observer seemed like shrewd thinking. Yet, I often find myself trying to juggle two jobs, three kids, and a house without ever asking for help of any kind.

So what explains the difference? Often we don't ask for help because we don't want to feel like we can't hack it. We don't place much of our identity in picnic table moving, but mothering is a different story. For me, this kind of dangerous no-help thinking often begins with a toxic comparison. I look at my friends who have even more on their plate. Then I launch into a series of unhealthy thoughts beginning with, "Well, if she can work, clean her own house, cook dessert every night, then what am I complaining about? I am such a wimp."

But the reality is that I can't do it all. In truth, I can do only about three-quarters of it even when I'm in top form. To get this job done, I need help. The more we can neutralize our irrational beliefs that prevent us from asking for help, the more likely we are to do it. By "neutralize" I mean disabuse ourselves of the notion that asking for help means we have somehow failed (or that we are lacking or that people will judge us or that we aren't good mothers). For many of us, this requires a shift in thinking. Rather than feeling that asking for help is evidence of our inadequacies, we need to remind ourselves that mothering demands a collective approach.

The type of help we as mothers require is quite varied. A young mother I work with expressed her great distress at having to accept government assistance to feed her children. At the same time, she knew she needed some help. She expressed her thinking beautifully when she said, "I thought proving that I was a good mother meant completely taking care of them myself with no help from anybody. But now I see that being a good mother means putting aside my pride and asking for things that I need." The same has been true for me. Instead of condemning myself for not being a more organized or capable mother, now when I need help, I ask the nearest person to *grab an end*. Not always, but more than before. The mantra *grab an end* helps me look at mothering as another form of heavy lifting. Asking for help isn't an indictment of my strength; it's taking a realistic view of the picnic table. Trying to lift without assistance is asking for a slipped disk.

• Resist the urge to resweep •

Another reason we have trouble asking for and accepting help is our unwillingness to relinquish control. My friend Alice told me the story of her mother hiring someone to help her with the housework after the birth of her fifth child. In addition to being a mother of five, she was also a full-time professor. Alice's mom was dead set against anyone coming in to help clean and agreed to it only under the condition that it was for a fixed period of time—until the baby was three months old. At that point she anticipated being back on her feet and returning to work. The night before the cleaning lady was supposed to come, Alice remembered going downstairs to get a glass of water and finding her mother vacuuming in anticipation of the cleaning lady's arrival. Rumor has it that she dusted, too. This went on for three months.

I have also found myself engaging in the double sweep, but on the back end. This is how it works in my home. It begins with me expressing my need for help around the house from the family, including my husband, our babysitter, and the kids. "After you eat, could someone please be responsible for sweeping up the floor?" As I return home from work, I urge myself to pay attention to the important things—how the children's days went, was the babysitter suicidal? But secretly I can't help glancing under the table. Did they sweep? Do I have to resweep? Rather than hurt people's feelings and resweep right in front of them, I wait until the end of the day and then clean the floor while feeling slightly sorry for myself. I might even lament that if you want it done right, you have to do it yourself. The martyr gig is particularly effective if you are down on your hands and knees in your best suit, wiping sticky juice off the floor with a damp sponge. You might even rationalize your behavior with the cry, "But we'll get ants (or roaches) if I don't do it!"

One night as I was chipping rice off the floor until my fingernails split, I realized I just might have a control issue. The problem was not that I wasn't getting help, because I was. It's just that the sweeping efforts of a well-meaning seven-year-old boy didn't match my military standards. I had become the crazy drill sergeant in movies, walking around with a white glove and bouncing quarters off of people's beds. Not really, but the point is that in an effort to gain control over what felt like an increasingly crazy life, I overfocused on the cleanliness of the floors. I have worked hard to develop impaired vision by squinting my eyes until I can't really see the dirt. Now when I come home, my husband whispers the mantra *resist the urge to resweep* as I scan the room. To some degree, asking for help means letting go. The mantra *resist the urge to resweep* encourages us to graciously accept help wherever it comes from and move on. Wrong brand of dish soap bought when someone helps with the shopping? No big deal. Laundry not folded in perfect quartiles? Who cares? Children fed ketchup and crackers for dinner by well-meaning grandparents? Thank the person profusely and go forward. What we lose in control when we *resist the urge to resweep*, we gain in letting others lighten our load.

A more serious note on getting help: There are times when we find ourselves overwhelmed and in need of more than a night out or an extra hand with the cleaning. If you find yourself unable to cope with the demands of mothering or turning to unhealthy means of managing your feelings, it may be that you need more than mantras. Mothering is not easy. In fact, it can be relentless, especially if you are trying to do it alone or under stressful circumstances. As mentioned elsewhere in this book, there are times when we need professional help or a consistently available support group to get us safely on the road to wellness. If you need this type of support, you certainly aren't alone. Whatever your situation is, asking for help sooner rather than later is a healthy choice for you and everyone you care for. *There is no health and sanity without your wellness.*

Chapter 20

• • •

Making Mistakes

Mothering offers many opportunities to screw up. Tonight at my son's baseball game I was chatting merrily with some people when up came a man holding a screaming two-year-old covered in mud. "*Who* is the mother of this baby?" he bellowed such that the umpire gave us a scornful look. "He's mine," I replied, walking over to retrieve him. "Well, do you know what he was doing? He was walking on that ledge *all by himself* and he fell into a pit of mud." The pathetic sight of my screaming child (who resembled something slightly larger than a chocolate-covered badger) triggered every self-condemning thought in my brain. The same night, another child (belonging to me) unintentionally smashed a friend's car with a baseball bat, leaving a healthy ding. Cause: lack of proper adult supervision. So much for moving to the country so that I didn't have to keep my eye on them every second.

As we drove home, I wondered where on the scale of screwing up do I fall? In the last six months I have let my cell phone disrupt the class play, much to the chagrin of the entire cast and audience. I have repeatedly forgotten my child's lunch, playdates, and library books' whereabouts. We missed the opening day of baseball. Spaced out on two birthday parties (yes, we have a calendar, but I was alternating between the calendar and the hang-the-flyer-on-the-fridge method). I wrote down the wrong date for the piano recital—missed it. I went out of town when I was supposed to chaperone the only field trip I signed up for. I often send them to school without their faces washed or teeth brushed. And last but not least, I went on vacation without my child's nebulizer—the possible outcome of which is death. Given the particulars, I feel safe in saying that I can speak to the issue of making mistakes with more authority than any other subject in this book. By the same token, my track record with mistakes has given rise to mantras to soften these experiences and make us wiser in their wake.

· We all make them ·

The mistakes listed above are fairly mundane. They float out of our consciousness shortly after they happen. But most of us have made the big ones as well—times when we said or did things harmful to our children. Perhaps these words or actions were expressed during a moment of stress. Or maybe they were reflexive, conditioned responses, but the damage they caused was undeniable. Recently I was revisiting Myla and Jon Kabat-Zinn's remarkable book *Everyday Blessings: The Inner Work of Mindful Parenting*. In a chapter entitled "Losing It," Myla tells a story of how at the end of a difficult night of trying to get her daughter to go to bed, she slapped her daughter on the cheek.

> Then I hear her sister yelling at us to be quiet. She's been woken up. I am even angrier now. I yell at her to be quiet. She continues to make noise and pound the bed and fuss, and I finally feel so frustrated and angry and helpless that I slap her on the cheek. She starts crying and then screaming even more loudly. Her sister yells again for her to be quiet. I feel sick that I've smacked her. She's shouting that I'm a child abuser and that she's going to call the police. I'm paralyzed with shame and remorse. I'm in the middle of a gigantic nightmare.

I hate to comb through this beautiful and elegant book only to surface with a story of how this mindful, intentional, loving mother slapped her daughter, but it illustrates the mantra perfectly. Even the most enlightened of us make mistakes. *We all make mistakes.* The essential (and healing) aspect of the story is what Myla did after committing an act she wished could undo. Rather than cut off from the painful feelings she experienced after the episode, including remorse, regret, shock, and disappointment, Myla took the time to look deeply into herself and the interaction. In doing so, she transformed the experience into a painful but vital opportunity to grow and learn. Myla writes, "As horrible as it is, there is usually *something* I can learn from this kind of wrenching experience that will make it easier to work with the next time something similar comes up."

In a sense, it's not about *what we do wrong* as much as *what we do next*. Myla first comforted her child by getting a cool cloth. Then she asked herself what she could have done differently, and what old reactive patterns were triggered by her daughter's behavior that resulted in the incident. Next, she apologized to her daughter without blaming or attacking her, and devised a plan to handle similar situations in the future. No matter how much mindfulness we try to bring to our mothering, we will falter. There's no way around it: *we all make mistakes.* But during those moments when you are convinced that no one makes mistakes as frequently or enormously as you, let the mantra remind you you're not alone.

· Good enough ·

Some professions thrive on perfection. I don't want my brain surgeon saying "Oops" and smiling sheepishly. I'd prefer my dry cleaner never use the wrong chemical or leave the iron down too long. It's excellent if the pharmacist doesn't leave a message on my machine that starts with, "Um, did you take any of that medicine yet?" But mothering is not a job in which perfection is possible or even desirable.

D. W. Winnicott was a British child psychiatrist in the 1950s and 1960s. Perhaps his greatest legacy to popular psychology has been the concept of the "ordinary devoted mother," later called the "good enough mother." Basically, Winnicott asserted that in the beginning of a baby's life, the ordinary devoted mother completely adapts to the needs of her child. In doing so, the baby comes to feel that he or she is *real* through this interaction with the mother. To the infant, there is no separate self. The mother and child are one. Winnicott writes: "We say that the mother's ego support facilitates the ego organization of the baby. Eventually the baby becomes able to assert his or her own individuality and even feel a sense of identity. The whole thing looks very simple when it goes well." Being an ordinary devoted mother in the early months simply means meeting all of the infant's physical and emotional needs as one would expect to do. No magic involved.

The risk, according to Winnicott, comes when a mother continues to meet all of the needs of the child once infancy has been outgrown. In the quest to become the perfect mother, she prevents him or her from experiencing the frustration, anger, and discomfort that come from functioning in the world. This, in turn, robs the child of an opportunity to master these difficult negative emotions. Further, by never allowing conflict to occur, the mother doesn't provide learning trials for the child to practice repairing emotional rifts in relationships. The good enough mother, on the other hand, is comfortable feeling negative emotions toward her child. Her attitude toward conflict with the child more resembles the *bring it on* mantra than *let's make nice*. Winnicott points out that far from being perfect, she isn't afraid to show a little "negative care" and "alive neglect" (see Hopkins 1996).

The mantra *good enough* is a reminder that perfectionism isn't necessarily something we should be shooting for in mothering. The times we screw up often offer us an opportunity to develop wisdom and insight. Our errors often provide our kids with a dose of resilience and self-sufficiency that they wouldn't have developed without growth-inducing challenges (aka our screwups). *Good enough* isn't meant to reinforce us when we hurt or harm our kids. It does ask us to reexamine how we view our human-ness. By asking for perfection from ourselves, what subtle mes-sages are we sending to our children? What tone does pressuring ourselves set for our families in terms of expectations, responses to failure, or one's worth as a human being? When I find myself losing sleep over my mistake-riddled mothering, I remind myself that in the long run, what I can muster is *good enough*.

· Back on the bull ·

There are periods of peacefulness and tranquillity in our home. Outings where there are no tears, reading in front of the fire without someone throwing very flammable things in just to see what will happen. Going to the beach usually goes well for us be-cause you can be naked (if you're under four or so) and as loud as you want. But there are times when mindful mothering feels like riding a mechanical bull. I am often thrown off—lying dazed on a sawdust floor. I feel beaten and remorseful about my lack of skill, patience, and understanding of my child. But then I realize that for as long as I'm on the floor beating myself up, no one is riding the bull (I'm not sure why that is important, but for the sake of the analogy it is). So I pick myself up and get *back on the bull*. I fall a lot, so I'm good at getting on mid-ride. To me, that's what mindful mothering boils down to—an unending commitment to getting *back on the bull*. After every mistake, the first thing I do is try to stop it from snowballing into a bigger error. I try to not wallow in my regret or start blaming my kids (more than they deserve) and jump *back on the bull*. I might not always be in control, but I am committed to the ride.

Chapter 21

. . .

Forgiving Ourselves

Mothering provides us with endless opportunities to practice the cycle of self-forgiveness, one which for me begins with a mistake, subsequent feelings of guilt and remorse, apologizing to a child, husband, teacher, or other person involved in my web of mothering, and finally freeing myself through self-forgiveness. As with any kind of forgiveness, self-forgiveness isn't a means of condoning acts that harm others. By practicing forgiveness we aren't saying that hurting your child is ever acceptable. In fact, self-forgiveness requires that we take *complete* responsibility for our actions. But within the process of self-forgiveness is the understanding that getting stuck in the guilt, remorse, or shame that often follows our mistakes is unproductive. It's like trying to mother with one hand tied behind your back. Self-forgiveness cuts the ropes so we can bring our whole selves back to the task of mothering.

⸱ Like it or not ⸱

Laura is one of the loveliest, most conscientious women I've had the luck to meet. She has two boys who are just as pleasant and sweet. One evening, Laura ran into the basement to check the laundry. Just as she opened the dryer, she heard a bloodcurdling shriek from the kitchen. From the minute she heard the pitch of the cry she knew it wasn't a simple swan dive from the couch. She ran upstairs, steeling herself for what she might find. And it was bad. Her youngest boy, Peter, had dragged a chair up to the stove. As he was climbing up, he pulled down a large pot of boiling water on himself. It was a traumatic accident for Peter, who required several skin grafts on his torso and arm over the course of the next three years. But it was equally emotionally devastating for Laura.

The guilt haunted her. She refused to speak about what happened with her family or husband. Internally, she berated herself and believed she was a careless, reckless mother. She withdrew emotionally from others, sure that they were judging her as harshly as she judged herself.

Finally, with her marriage strained and her children buckling under the burden of their mother's pain, she agreed to talk to a therapist about Peter's accident. After encouraging Laura to express her feelings of anger and sorrow, the therapist helped Laura reframe it for what it was—a horrible confluence of events that might have happened to any one of us. Over time, Laura began letting go of her intense guilt. Each time she condemned herself, her therapist asked her to say a mantra reminding her that being forgiven was a done deal. The mantra is derived from theologian Father Thomas Hopko, who states, "We are forgiven whether we like it or not." By nature of who we are, because the core Self is innocent and good, we are forgiven already.

When she heard the mantra *like it or not*, something clicked in Laura. Despite her progress in letting go of the guilt, part of her *didn't like* the idea of forgiving herself. Laura had a lot of reasons for taking this position. First and foremost, she felt that she didn't really deserve to be forgiven. If Peter had to live with his scars, then she should also bear a permanent burden. Also, by holding on to the guilt, she felt like she was making sure that nothing like this would ever happen again. She told herself that her guilt and "wrongness" kept her on her toes. However, Laura could see that her refusal to surrender her self-blame was holding her back from being completely available to her children. The mantra *like it or not* was the gentle push that Laura needed to begin forgiving herself.

Self-forgiveness is a process. It's not like we reach some mountaintop and find that the quest is over. Laura still felt periodic moments of anger toward herself and the world for the accident. Often we must extend forgiveness toward ourselves over and over again. Each time we practice self-forgiveness, we are asking ourselves to look differently at who we really are. When we choose to see with self-forgiveness we see the good, peaceful, wise fundamental nature instead of the hurt or angry "smaller self" we have been caught in. It might take a great deal of time to be able to offer ourselves genuine forgiveness. But *like it or not*, we have already received it. *Like it or not*, we are forgiven as mothers and as people. When I get lost in self-judgment, guilt, or anger toward myself, the mantra *like it or not* is a reminder that nothing is gained by beating myself up over and over. The sooner I can begin the process of self-forgiveness, the sooner I fully come back to myself and to my children. The mantra *like it or not* reminds me of this logic.

Part Five

The Mommy Trifecta:
Perspective, Flexibility,
and Humor

In horse racing, of which I am a denizen (not really, but my grandfather used to sneak me into the track when I was a little girl), a trifecta happens when a bettor selects the win, place, and show horses in the correct order. When this happens, you have had yourself a good day at the ponies. In terms of mothering (or living, really), the big three cognitive or attitudinal powerhouses are the abilities to put any given situation into a larger perspective, deal with whatever gets thrown at you, and laugh at yourself, your kids, and the world. When I can get all three of these skills running at full capacity, I know I've had a good day of mothering. I feel like donning roses around my neck and taking a victory lap. Or at the very least wallowing in good champagne.

Just like with a racing trifecta, we don't always get all three horses across the line in one day (forget about in the right order). Sometimes the best we can do is sit back in the evening after a mind-warping day and put things in perspective. You might pep yourself up with, "Well, *at least* no one lost a leg." I am also fond of fooling myself into thinking that quitting is actually its more adaptive cousin, flexibility. "Oh, you think we should have marshmallows and fudge for dinner rather than baked cod? Excellent idea!"

But sometimes we're really on. Like a fine athlete, be it horse or human, we find our stride. All engines are firing at once. It happened this morning. I was late for work when my daughter blew a gasket. We had just reminded her that today was open house for visiting her new class in school. Instead of cheerfully picking out a special outfit with a joyous heart and trilling voice, she screamed, "I will never, ever go to that place again." When my daughter gets very upset, she actually foams at the mouth. And this was the case today. Next she crumpled on the bed in tears. My initial reaction was to see her volume and raise her ten decibels. But I took a deep breath, put the situation in perspective (annoying yes, but not a catastrophe), adopted a flexible stance (as in, I will not be on time for work), and sat with her through it. I barely escaped following my first impulse to give her a stern look and inform her that the car was leaving in ten minutes and that we could do it the easy way or the hard way. Had I taken this approach, though understandable, we would have been stuck in the starting gate. I wouldn't have heard how sad she was about leaving her old school and how much she missed New York City since moving a year ago. I wouldn't have heard her talk about the friends she left behind and the fact that her new home still didn't feel like home.

After she was done " 'spressin' herself," she wiped the tears from her face, smiled, and left to get dressed. I sat there for a minute, stunned and bemused. Did she really miss the old downstairs neighbor—a retired fellow who despised us and banged on the ceiling with a broom? Beats me. But stepping back, I was able to laugh (ironically) that we sacrificed our careers and friendships to raise them in a house with a lawn, which they loathe. As I watched her leave the room, I didn't feel flooded by stress or angry that I was so late. Being in the mothering flow (thanks to the trifecta) ultimately left me feeling more in control than if I had stormed out of the house and been at work on time. It was one of those rare occasions when I felt like I got it right. A challenge of mothering had been lobbed my way, and I knocked it out of the park.

Getting it all to line up is a rarity for me, akin to winning a real trifecta. But I dramatically increase the likelihood of intentional and mindful mothering when I can put things in perspective, act flexibly, and bring humor to the job. Unlike a complete gamble, just by choosing to practice the skills and attitudes of the mommy trifecta, I've already bumped up my odds of winning some semblance of sanity (or at least breaking even).

Chapter 22

. . .

Perspective

. Stand behind the yellow line .

When I first moved to a major metropolitan area from the hinter-lands, I was stunned by the faith the city placed in its populace. Over and over I asked myself, "Why do they let people get so dangerously close to the subway cars? Shouldn't there be a rail or something?" One good shove from a disgruntled straphanger and hello, third rail. I would marvel as people teetered near the edge of the platform while the wind current rearranged their hairdos. I was terrified and stunned by the whole experience. A person seemed so vulnerable, and scant warnings were issued other than a barely visible yellow line running along the platform. Strangely enough, when I became a mother I noticed strong parallels between the two situations; there are few indicators as to the real perils of the enterprise, and every ten minutes or so the possibility of a head-on collision arises. Given the similarities between standing on a subway platform and mothering, it isn't surprising that the solution to managing them is the same—when something is coming down the track, stand back. Not as in turn tail and run away from the situation, but take a few steps back in order to get some perspective.

My friend Lena recently stopped answering the phone; rather, she started screening her calls. Toward the end of the year, she would get a call two or three times a week from her seven-year-old son's teacher saying that he was too loud, wasn't following class rules, and wasn't completing all of his work. Lena and her husband spoke to Chris about the calls. They had conferences with the teacher and gave consequences each time she reported another incident. Lena was growing more and more frustrated and alarmed. She felt that her son was spiraling out of control and feared he was headed intractably down the wrong path. Soon he would smoke cigarettes and drive around all night with the bad boys, the outcasts. The last straw came when he told a lunch lady who asked why he was dancing and hopping while in line that his penis was itchy. Apparently, this caused the woman to have some sort of near-death experience. This time the principal called home.

As Lena cried at the kitchen table, her mother-in-law said, "You know, dear, I don't want to interfere and I agree that Chris should behave in class, but his father was the same way. He was always acting foolish in school. But he turned out just fine. [Read: quite successful professionally, never ran away, tattooed every inch of his body, or joined the circus.] I think everyone might be making a mountain out of a molehill." As her mother-in-law spoke, Lena could see that with each call, she had stepped closer and closer to the train until she had lost all perspective. Lena decided that she needed to *stand behind the yellow line* to see the bigger picture and to balance her own emotional response to the situation. Lena talked to Chris and was convinced that his actions had been those of a naive seven-year-old with an itchy penis, not of a depraved sociopath attempting to scar the lunch lady's psyche.

Lena's shift in attitude didn't mean that Chris suddenly had free rein. However, in stepping back, Lena could see that the fatigue brought on by the end of the school year had constricted people's vision. They had all lost perspective. Now when the phone rings, she answers it but is careful to *stand behind the yellow line*. Rather than allowing each call to serve as proof that her son is heading for reform school, Lena steps back and sees an energetic, ebullient, sweet-hearted kid who has trouble sitting still for three-hour blocks of time and sometimes says goofy things.

It's often difficult to get instant perspective on situations as mothers. Things happen fast and we're emotionally charged. But with practice, we can establish a tendency to regularly *stand behind the yellow line*. In doing so, we begin to see that the gravity and oppressiveness of situations are magnified when we have tunnel vision. When we *stand behind the yellow line*, we realize that whatever has us torn up inside likely isn't the end of the world. We can see the train for what it really is. By stepping back, we change our relationship to it. All of a sudden it isn't so loud or perilous. In fact, like many challenges, it will probably end up taking us somewhere even if we didn't want to go in the first place.

. . .

Chapter 23

Flexibility

. Try the wrench .

I am not a flexible thinker, and this has worked against me my
whole life. As proof, I offer the incident when I was eight years
old, trying to get the chain off my bike with a screwdriver. I
hacked and hacked at it until grease and blood mixed on my tiny
forearms. My mother walked by and with her gentle wisdom
suggested, "Maybe you should try a wrench." I looked at the nut

on the end of the threaded bolt and thought, "Ah, the wrench." Perfectly logical solution, which would never have occurred to me in a million years. I knew what a wrench was. Had used one in the past. But I was locked into solving this problem with the one tool I had carried out from the pantry.

So what is cognitive flexibility? Neuropsychologist Francisco Barcelo and his colleagues define it as a "readiness to direct attention to novel events and an ability to change one's mental set to find new solutions for old problems." Or, in mantra talk—*try the wrench*. Unfortunately, this trait of cognitive inflexibility has followed me into adulthood and has undermined my mothering on many occasions. One task that has always brought my inflexibility out in full force is trying to ensnare children (particularly toddlers) in car seats or strollers. There is something about the stiffening of their bodies into tiny surfboards that spurs me to forcibly stuff them in with an elbow while fastening buckles with the other hand. My take-no-prisoners attitude, in turn, prompts the child to begin screaming at the top of his or her lungs and thrashing. I believe it's similar to how an animal must feel when it realizes that its foot is caught in a trap. Some animals will bite their own leg off to escape. My children have come close. These struggles leave me exhausted and frazzled.

The other day I watched my husband buckle our two-year-old into the car seat. True to form, the child started to resist captivity. Instead of pinning him down with his even larger elbow, my husband adopted a freaky high-pitched voice and began chiming, "Look, look, a giant yellow bird is there behind the bush." We all froze and tried to crane our necks around. Where was this bird? Our son immediately stopped fighting for his life and switched his attention to locating this mythical fowl. In seconds, the child was buckled in and we were headed down the road. My husband kept asking questions about the mystery bird to keep the kid from realizing he'd been restrained. "Did you see him? Oh, he was a big one, all right. What sound does a bird that big make?" I sat back in my seat, appreciating his brilliance. Rather than fighting them for all these years, I could have been distracting the tykes. I then started to count up the thousands of buckling battles I have engaged in over the course of my mothering that might have been avoided if I had been flexible enough to *try the wrench*.

Those of you who read the above story and decided that I must be a total idiot for not trying another solution to this relatively straightforward problem are probably the same mothers I watch enviably as they flexibly shift gears to avoid their kids' meltdowns. For some, flexible thinking and fluid problem-solving approaches are second nature. However, for the more cognitively rigid among us, it helps to have a mantra like *try the wrench*, which suggests there may be another way of handling a situation, whether it's a new problem or one we come up against again and again. *Try the wrench* reminds us to think flexibly and open ourselves up to a wider range of solutions. It's the mothering equivalent of thinking outside the box.

Hopefully by this point you've found that using mantras, if nothing else, can shift our mood in a positive direction. This is important given the new research showing that positive affect (or mood) significantly increases our cognitive flexibility. Essentially, the less angry or agitated we are, the more efficient our brains are at problem solving. This is definitely true for me. I have long noticed that during a conflict with a child, the more emotionally fraught I get, the more rigid my thinking becomes. I'm hacking at the chain with a screwdriver once again. But the mantra *try the wrench* reminds me that there is more than one way to skin a cat. And some of the solutions are far more pleasant than others, I would imagine. Now each time I approach the stroller or the car seat, I *try the wrench*. If that doesn't work, there's always the pliers.

Chapter 24

· · ·

Humor

· Pop the cork ·

The last member of the trifecta family is humor. Unlike the two
other horses (perspective and flexibility), which can be used in
the thick of battle, humor often comes across the finish line long
after the crowds have gone home. There are times, no matter
how hard I try, when things just don't seem funny in the moment. If I could find humor in these situations, I wouldn't need

a mantra. When my seven-year-old was caught biting his toenails off with his teeth because he wanted to do it "the old fashion way," we laughed. We needed a camera so we could embarrass him at his wedding, not a mantra. When he got lost in a super-market that resembled a combination of Disneyland, a giant corn maze, and a food warehouse, we needed humor to put ourselves back together again.

Researchers have known for decades the positive psychological and physiological effects of humor and laughter. Studies have shown that high levels of humor are associated with increased self-esteem, less depressive symptomology, lowered negative af-fective response to stress, and reductions in physical arousal. Laughter has been shown to bolster the immune system and re-duce blood pressure. One of the primary ways that humor helps us cope is by allowing us to reframe stressful events and provide a sense of "distance" from them. By adopting a humorous per-spective, we transform the way we *see* things, which shifts how we *feel* about them. Norman Cousins was a pioneer in humor re-search who attributed his remarkable cure from ankylosing spondylitis to high doses of vitamin C and the daily viewing of funny movies. If it can bring a man back from a lethal illness, imagine the effects humor might have on a stressed-out mother.

Shortly after children become ambulatory in New York City, we teach them the valuable lesson of what to do if they get lost. Paradoxically, children are rarely actually lost in New York City, because most mothers are hypervigilant with fear. There may be slight variations in the lecture, but the main points are usually similar: Stay where you are; call to me using my first name, not "Mommy"; and if I don't find you in a few minutes, find a woman with children, tell her that you are lost, and calmly recite my cell phone number. Periodically, I would give my eldest surprise quizzes. I went so far as to ask him to recall my phone number when he was stressed out in an attempt to see how he would react under pressure. I was fairly confident in his mastery of the drill. Plus, he was completely paranoid about getting lost and never let me stray from his line of vision.

So, when I saw no sign of him in the large sprawling theme park of a supermarket we were in, my heart froze. Abduction was the only logical answer. I began screaming his name at the top of my lungs and running frantically through the disorienting maze of aisles. I found a store employee, who located a manager. Per store policy, all points of entrance and egress were closed. Nobody was coming in and nobody was going out until the child was located. Walkie-talkies were engaged. Then the dreaded over-the-intercom announcement was made describing the make and model of the missing child. ("Mother *cannot* recall color of his shirt," they were nice enough to disclose.) At this point I started to cry. He could be stuffed in a trunk and near the state line by now. Before the catastrophizing could really get rolling, I saw my son round the corner escorted by a giant bipedal cow and a man who looked like the national representative of the Hell's Angels (not that bikers can't be gentle guardians, as this one was). I looked at my son and cried louder when I saw his ashen face. I did not find this funny—at all.

After we all calmed down, we asked him why he broke every single rule in the charter. Why, oh why, did he start running as fast as possible from the last known whereabouts of his parents the second he realized he was lost? Rather than finding a woman who looked like an incarnation of Mary, mother of God with kids, why did he choose a talking cow and a biker? And why didn't he ask anyone to call my cell? His answer was reasonable though highly unsatisfying. "I forgot," he sobbed.

Later that night my husband sat at the table revisiting the incident. The grimness of the afternoon hadn't fully dissipated. We were both still shaken and wrapped up with dark thoughts of what could have happened. Then my husband looked at me and said, "Why did he go for the cow? He's afraid of cows." As soon as we thought about the vision of our child walking down the aisle sandwiched between his two unlikely rescuers, we laughed until tears ran down our faces. Just like when we shake a bottle of champagne and then *pop the cork*, all the built-up pressure we had been carrying around escaped. Without naming names, one of us might have peed in her pants thinking about the absurdity of the situation. Each time we told the story, we laughed again. Sometimes harder than the first time we *popped the cork*, depending on the audience. As we laughed, we felt a greater sense of distance from the gut-wrenching experience of losing our kid. In telling the story over and over, we moved into the driver's seat rather than being blindfolded and hijacked by fear. Eventually, most of the residual feelings of fear, distress, and dread were drained from the event, leaving just the funny parts.

As an aside, if you can use humor in the midst of mothering madness, you are in for the bonus trifecta. Research conducted by Alice Isen at Cornell University shows that positive affect (and humor would induce such a state) enhances one's cognitive flexibility and increases problem-solving capabilities. We've all had our go with the self-defeating spiral: when we are in a bad mood, thinking becomes constricted and rigid, we become angrier that the problem is not getting fixed, and eventually someone has a tantrum. Conversely, Isen found that "people in positive affect are 'open-minded,' unbiased, responsive to input and requirements of the situation." A far cry from beating your head against a rock like I tend to do when mothering from a funk. If you can, lighten up. If the research is right, the wrench will be easier to find.

But we can't always *pop a cork* and have a gut laugh about every difficult event in our lives. Sometimes the best we can manage is a shake of the head as we reflect on the irony of a situation (which is often the seed state of humor). Furthermore, our ability to see humor or levity may require some time to pass.

But any small motion we make toward reframing our trials through humor is a step in the right direction. Each time we laugh (or shudder with a grimace), we allow the stress of mothering to dissipate. The mantra *pop the cork* reminds us of the restorative capacity that humor holds. Nothing revives a beat-down, exhausted mother like a good laugh.

Sometimes at the end of the night I climb the stairs and muse, "Are you kidding me with this?" I pass my statue of Buddha and look at his grin. Buddha, knowing the truth of our existence, is often depicted as smiling, as though he's on the verge of laughing. I look at his face and imagine that he's seen what transpired during my day as a mother and is chuckling at it all with great compassion, reminding me each night to laugh away the stress and craziness so that the next day can begin with a clean slate. *Pop the cork* is my reminder that maybe he's on to something.

Epilogue

As I began writing this book I asked my mother how she knew what to do when it came to mothering. I'm not sure what I was fishing for. Maybe something that included lines like "handed down through the generations" or "Well, honey, in those days . . ." or "At your birth, it was like a little microphone had been placed in my ear, telling me right from wrong." Her response was not the comforting wealth of wisdom I had antici-pated. "Um, for the most part, I just made it up as I went." I left the conversation wishing for a more definitive answer, but it's true. We go on gut, a quick check with the pundits, but mostly by the seat of our pants. When it comes to mothering, by and large *we make it up*. No matter what kind of expert you are or how many kids you have, there's a lot of winging it involved.

We encourage adopting the same approach to this book. By all means, while reading it, take as yours anything that strikes a chord. But when it comes to finding a mantra that really works for you, if it's not here, *make it up*. This book would have been a short read had it not been for the mantras of our friends, fam-ily, and some forthright strangers. In fact, most of the really good ones we stole from someone else. If at the end of the day mak-ing up mantras, like brushing your teeth, requires too much ef-fort, then steal them like we did. Where the mantra comes from is far less important than what it does in terms of transforming your outlook, increasing your tolerance for the job, and giving you the determination to get *back on the bull* for another day of mindful mothering.

Acknowledgments

As with everything in our lives, this book would never have come into existence without the unflagging support and love of our families. The generosity and care of our husbands are unparalleled. Newt selflessly served as sounding board, kid wrangler, and chief chef as we hammered away at the keyboard. Peter listened endlessly to ideas, plans, and visions, and helped find balance and laughter in the midst of chaos. We thank our parents, Suzan Lawlor Huebner, Zsuzsa and Charles Huebner, Linnette

Gushee, and Zaven Casarjian, for being steadfast sources of inspiration, creativity, and unconditional acceptance. Robin Casarjian read endless versions of the manuscript and provided invaluable guidance for this project. Her ideas and teachings are present throughout this book.

We want to thank all of our siblings and their spouses for the love and torture they have shown us over the years. This project would never have evolved without Samantha Skey and Greg Dillon's early involvement. We are eternally grateful to Amanda Casarjian, whose research skills far exceed our own and whose support is an act of true love.

Wonderful in-laws Monika and Brian Dillon provided generous and loving care to their grandchildren so we could develop and teach this material at the Omega Institute. Shamelly Vega has been part of the Casarjian/Davis family for the last five years, and without her warmth, humor, and gift for keeping the peace we would never have been able to sit down long enough to write this book. Doris Estevez has given endless hours of loving and patient care to the Dillon kids. And of course we thank our exuberant, wonderful, awe-inspiring children for giving us the opportunity to do the one thing we cherish above all else—be their mothers.

We extend our deepest appreciation to Anne Dunn, whose brilliant editorial skills have seen Beth through two books. Our agent Ned Leavitt was a pure joy to collaborate with, and we are grateful for his creativity, insight, and moral support. Patricia

Medved, our editor, believed in this book from its inception, and her enthusiasm and vision were lights in the fog. We are grateful to Courtney Nichols, who paved the way for Mommy Mantras to be launched at the Omega Institute, and Courtney Martin for contribution to early incantations of the idea. We'd also like to thank Diane's colleagues at The School at Columbia University for their unwavering support at every stage of the project. Elizabeth Brady, Jeff DeTeso, and Dr. Albert Ellis laid important groundwork.

We offer many thanks to friends who were generous enough with their time to read earlier chapters of the book. Dr. Marla Brassard, longtime friend and esteemed professor at Teacher's College, Columbia University, reassured us once again that we were headed down the right track and hadn't mangled the facts. Sascha Griffing, Ph.D., let us chew up hours of her time as we tried to find the right lines of logic.

We want to express our profound gratitude to our dear friends from whom we learned, in large part, how to mother and who saved our sanity on the many occasions when mantras weren't enough: Linda, Michele, Denise, Jennifer, Penny, Julia, Jeanne, Cécile, Dorie, Lesley, Aleece, Beth, Becky, Matthew, Jill, Chrissy, and Miriam. Finally, we'd like to offer our sincere appreciation to the hundreds of mothers who have shared their intimate stories and companionship with us. It is our wish that your wisdom, patience, and humor will provide other mothers the same relief it gave us.

References

Introduction
Walen, S., DiGiuseppe, R., and Dryden, W. *A Practitioner's Guide to Rational-Emotive Therapy*. New York: Oxford University Press, 1992.

Chapter 1
Goleman, D. *Emotional Intelligence: Why It Can Matter More Than IQ*. New York: Bantam Books, 1995.

Chapter 2
Werner, E., and Smith, R. *Overcoming the Odds: High Risk Children from Birth to Adulthood*. Ithaca, N.Y.: Cornell University Press, 1992.

Chapter 3
Tolle, E. *The Power of Now: A Guide to Spiritual Enlightenment*. Novoto, Cal.: New World Library, 1999.

Chapter 6
Childre, D., and Martin, H. *The HeartMath Solution*. San Francisco: HarperSanFrancisco, 1999.

Chapter 7
Brach, T. *Radical Acceptance: Embracing Your Life with the Heart of a Buddha*. New York: Bantam Books, 2003.

Goleman, D. *Destructive Emotions: How Can We Overcome Them? A Scientific Dialogue with the Dalai Lama*. New York: Bantam Books, 2003.

Rosenthal, R., and Jacobson, L. *Pygmalion in the Classroom: Teacher Expectation and Pupils' Intellectual Development*. New York: Holt, Rinehart and Winston, 1968.

Babad, E., and Taylor, P. "Transparency of Teacher Expectations Across Language and Cultural Boundaries." *Journal of Educational Research* **86** (1992): 120–25.

Chapter 9
Bandura, A. *Social Learning Theory*. Englewood Cliffs, N.J.: Prentice-Hall, 1977.

Chapter 11
Casarjian, R. *Forgiveness: A Bold Choice for a Peaceful Heart*. New York: Bantam Books, 1992.

Chapter 12
Carter, B., and McGoldrick, M. (eds.) *The Changing Family Life Cycle: A Framework for Family Therapy*. Boston: Allyn and Bacon, 1989.

The Dalai Lama and Hatier, F. *The Dalai Lama's Little Book of Inner Peace*. New York: Barnes and Noble, 2002.

Chapter 13
Bank, S., and Kahn, M. *The Sibling Bond.* New York: Basic Books, 1982.

Fraiberg, S., Adelson, E., and Shapiro, V. "Ghosts in the Nursery: A Psychoanalytic Approach to the Problems of the Impaired Infant-Mother Relationship." *Journal of the American Academy of Child Psychiatry* **14** (1975): 387–421.

Chapter 14
Gottman, J. *Why Marriages Succeed or Fail and How You Can Make Yours Work.* New York: Simon and Schuster, 1994.

Lee, Y. S., and Waite, L. "Husbands' and Wives' Time Spent on Housework: A Comparison of Measures." *Journal of Marriage and Family* **67** (2005): 328–36.

Kabat-Zinn, J. *Wherever You Go There You Are: Mindfulness Meditation in Everyday Life.* New York: Hyperion, 1994.

Part Four
Trungpa, C. *The Heart of the Buddha.* Boston: Shambhala, 1991.

Chapter 15
Kornfield, J. *After the Ecstasy, the Laundry.* New York: Bantam Books, 2000.

Wells, A. "Variations in Mothers' Self-Esteem in Daily Life." *Journal of Personality and Social Psychology* **55** (1988): 661–68.

Rinpoche, S. *The Tibetan Book of Living and Dying.* San Francisco: HarperSanFrancisco, 1992.

Bodian, S. *Meditation for Dummies.* Foster City, Cal.: IDG Books, 1999.

Grossman, P., Niemann, L., Schmidt, S., and Walach, H. "Mindfulness-Based Stress Reduction and Health Benefits: A Meta-Analysis." *Journal of Psychosomatic Research* **57** (2004): 35–43.

Kabat-Zinn, J. *Wherever You Go There You Are: Mindfulness Meditation in Everyday Life.* New York: Hyperion, 1994.

Chapter 16

Walen, S., DiGiuseppe, R., and Dryden, W. *A Practitioner's Guide to Rational-Emotive Therapy.* New York: Oxford University Press, 1992.

Dodge, K., and Somberg, D. "Hostile Attributional Biases Among Aggressive Boys Are Exacerbated Under Conditions of Threat to Self." *Child Development* **58** (1987): 213–24.

Dodge. K., and Frame, C. "Social Cognitive Biases and Deficits in Aggressive Boys." *Child Development* **53** (1982): 620–35.

Kornfield, J. *After the Ecstasy, the Laundry.* New York: Bantam Books, 2000.

Baumeister, R., and Twenge, J. "The Social Self." In Millon, T., and Lerner, M. (eds.), *Handbook of Psychology: Personality and Social Psychology*, vol. 5. New York: John Wiley and Sons, Inc., 2003.

Chapter 17

Larson, R., and Richards, M. *Divergent Realities: The Emotional Lives of Mothers, Fathers and Adolescents.* New York: Basic Books, 1994.

Rinpoche, S. *The Tibetan Book of Living and Dying.* San Francisco: HarperSanFrancisco, 1992.

Csikszentmihalyi, M. *Flow: The Psychology of Optimal Experience.* New York: Harper Perennial, 1991.

Chapter 20

Kabat-Zinn, M., and Kabat-Zinn, J. *Everyday Blessings: The Inner Work of Mindful Parenting.* New York: Hyperion, 1997.

Winnicott, D. W. *Winnicott on the Child.* Cambridge, Mass: Perseus Publishing, 2002.

Hopkins, J. "The Dangers and Deprivations of Too Good Mothering." *Journal of Child Psychotherapy* **22** (1996): 407–22.

Hopko, T. "Living in Communion: An Interview with Father Thomas Hopko." *Parabola* **12** (1987).

Chapter 23
Barcelo, F., Perianez, J., and Knight, R. "Think Differently: A Brain Orienting Response to Task Novelty." *NeuroReport* **13** (2002): 1887–92.

Isen, A. "Missing in Action in the AIM: Positive Affect's Facilitation of Cognitive Flexibility, Innovation, and Problem Solving." *Psychological Inquiry* **13** (2002): 29–89.

Abel, M. "Humor, Stress, and Coping Strategies." *Humor* 15 (2002): 365–81.

Martin, R. "Sense of Humor and Physical Health: Theoretical Issues, Recent Findings, and Future Directions." *Humor* **17** (2004): 1–19.

ABOUT THE AUTHORS

Bethany Casarjian is a mother of three and the clinical director of the National Emotional Literacy Project for Youth at Risk. She lives in Weston, Massachusetts.

Diane Dillon is a mother of two and the director of the Child Study Team at The School at Columbia University. She lives in New York City.

Both authors are psychologists who work with children and families.

Buster's Diaries

Buster's Diaries

AS TOLD TO ROY HATTERSLEY

Deputy Prime Minister in previous Socialist Government — about 20 years ago.

Illustrations by Chris Riddell

LITTLE, BROWN AND COMPANY

A *Little, Brown* Book

Published by Little, Brown 1998

Reprinted 1998 (twice)

Copyright © Roy Hattersley 1998

Text illustrations copyright © Chris Riddell 1998

The moral right of the author has been asserted

A CIP catalogue record for this book is
available from the British Library

ISBN 0 316 64592 3

Typeset in Berkeley by M Rules
Printed and bound in Great Britain by
The Bath Press, Bath

Little, Brown and Company (UK)
Brettenham House
Lancaster Place
London WC2E 7EN

Introduction

My brother and I were born in the overgrown back garden of a house in Paddington sometime during February 1995. When we were a few days old, our mother was bitten by a rat and the man who owned her tied her to a fence post and left her to die. For nearly a week, she survived on water which was leaking from a hose pipe and she fed us till she died. Then Diana, the lady who lived next door, rescued us. Being too young and stupid to recognise kindness, after a couple of weeks we ran away and started to live rough. It was the beginning of my fascination with refuse. Even now, with two square meals a day and more biscuits than are good for me, I find black bags and waste bins irresistible.

We had been vagrants for more than two months, when Doris Turner saw us running about on Paddington Recreation Ground. Doris ran the Brent Animal Shelter and decided at once that she must find us a good home. Even then, for reasons I can't explain, I longed for human company. So, when Doris called to us, I let her catch me. My brother, being still stupid, ran away again. It was the last time I saw him. Doris said he was my identical twin. Somewhere in North London, there is another dog who looks just like me – the handsome profile of a small Alsatian and the elegant brown and gold flecked coat of a Staffordshire Bull Terrier.

Doris was the first person who ever talked to me. Often I could not understand what she tried to say. But despite that I liked to listen to the noise she made. Now I understand much more – although I still have difficulty with complicated

3

sentences, especially if they are spoken in a conversational tone. I have a particular problem with subjunctives. But whenever someone speaks to me, I feel happy. Conversation was, I suppose, the beginning of my corruption – or domestication, as humans call it.

Talk is now the noise I hear most often. Because of that, the wolf within me sleeps – although he sometimes dreams. It was the wolf who kept me alive on the Paddington Recreation Ground, but when he dreams, we go back together to the Siberian forest, not to north London. These days I would not swap my bed against the radiator for a patch of frozen moss under a stunted tree. But I am glad that the wolf is still there, snoring away inside me.

When Doris found me, the wolf was still wide awake and I had not yet learnt that a dog has to choose between the luxury of family life and the excitement of the wild. So I expected to live with Doris for ever, listening to her talk when the mood took me and fighting for my life the rest of the time. But Doris, who was old, thought I needed more exercise than she could organise. So she found me a foster home in a flat a couple of roads away from her house. My new owners did their best to burn off my energy. But I didn't settle down. Sheila – a 'home-checker' for the RSPCA and Battersea – said I 'lacked socialisation skills with both dogs and humans'. I was taken into canine care. Doris and her friends paid the fees.

The people who ran the dogs' home kept me warm and well fed. But they did not talk to me. Indeed, they did not talk